At home in Renvyle

Recipes by Tim O'Sullivan   Illustrations by Róisín Coyle

At home

A CIP catalogue record for
this book is available from the
British Library.

ISBN: 978 1 897685 71 6

Published 2005 by
Onstream Publications Ltd.
Currabaha, Cloghroe,
County Cork Ireland.

Tel 353 21 4385798
website: www.onstream.ie
email: info@onstream.ie.

  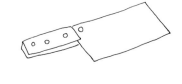

in Renvyle

Editor
Roz Crowley

Book design and production
Tony O'Hanlon Propeller, Galway

Photography
Petra Carter 41, 44, 65, 70, 77, 86, 104, 118, 123, 124, 125 and cover
Zoë Fitzgerald 6. 7, 13, 29, 31, 43, 69, 83, 89
Paul Sherwood 3, 17, 23, 32, 36, 51, 53, 55, 63, 73, 75, 78

Print
Nicholson & Bass

The scenery is enough to seduce at Renvyle, but when a day out in the wilds of Connemara is followed by a meal cooked by Tim O'Sullivan, it becomes something close to perfection.

With a reputation that has grown organically, Tim has been in no rush to be a star chef and is slow to put himself into the limelight. He just likes to cook. Fellow chefs admire his lack of ego and down to earth attitude to cooking and his attention to what many forget – the pure taste of good food. That is not to say that Tim's dishes are anything but stylish on the plate, but taste is never sacrificed to pretty pictures. In his twenty-two years there, he has worked with the best local produce, supplementing it with a touch of the exotic, a touch of classic Mediterranean, to produce exceptional dishes he can call his own.

In this book you will find no silly pretensions or attempts to make recipes sound difficult to enhance his mystique, so all of them are accessible to cooks who like to take just a little trouble for guests and themselves. The more complicated dishes can be simplified by cutting out the side dishes and sauces and using Tim's methods for the core ingredient. However, beware, when you get a good result, you will be seduced into going the whole way, and what's more you will enjoy the process. Where it is possible to prepare ahead, I have given notes and ideas for short-cuts approved by Tim, but which he would not use for his valued clients. He is a purist. His stocks are well worth making and are the basis for many of his excellent soups, sauces and gravies, and their intensity is a hallmark of his style.

Renvyle House has an interesting history. Donal O'Flaherty, one of the chieftains of Ireland's most powerful clans in the province of Connaught lived there, and Augustus John painted some portraits which were burned when the hotel was razed to the ground in 1923. This was during the tenure of Oliver St. John Gogarty who, having wound down his medical practice, bought Renvyle as a country residence. During this time and later when it opened again for paying guests, luminaries such as WB Yeats, Denis Johnston, 'the Pope' O'Mahony, Count and Countess McCormack, Lord and Lady Longford, Mr and Mrs Churchill, Lord and Lady Glenavy and Stephen Gwynn signed the guest register.

Writers Somerville and Ross enjoyed their time in the house and wrote about it later, like so many literary figures that were inspired there. It was quite the place to relax, as it is today.

In 1952 Gogarty sold it to Dr Donny Coyle and friends; his son John Coyle owns it now and continues the strong tradition of hospitality and hosting of an eclectic clientele. Guests stay for whatever appeals to them most, but Tim O'Sullivan's food must be top of the list of attractions.

This is a book to take to bed and remember or wish for a holiday or an overnight stay at Renvyle. The recipes work, that's for sure, and a handful of well-chosen ingredients, used with a light hand, will stimulate the senses and bring a heady enjoyment - all of which we can hope for with good food, especially at Renvyle.

ROZ CROWLEY, EDITOR

FIRST COURSES AND LUNCH DISHES

14	Connemara Mussels with Lemongrass and Ginger
15	Angel Hair Pasta with Killary Bay Prawns
16	Tower of Crabmeat, Won Ton Pastry, Mixed Salad Leaves and Spring Onion Salsa
19	Chicken Mousse with Tarragon
20	Chicken Liver Paté
21	Mozzarella and Grilled Tomato Salad
22	Springroll of Duck with Spicy Stir Fried Vegetables, Pineapple and Spring Onion Salsa and Savoury Couscous
24	Goat's Cheese, Rocket and Red Pepper Salsa
25	Renvyle Salad with Smoked Tuna
26	Connemara Smoked Fish Platter
27	West Coast Crab Cakes with Coriander, Coconut and Curry Cream
28	Roulade of the Sea with Cream Cheese, Mixed Salad Leaves and Curried Crème Fraîche

SOUPS

33	Oyster Soup
34	Mushroom Soup
35	Cauliflower and Almond Soup
37	Apple and Onion Soup
38	Carrot and Orange Soup
39	Broccoli and Blue Cheese Soup
40	Seafood Chowder
42	Asparagus Soup

MAIN COURSES

Fish	45-46	Pan-Seared Sea Bass, Basil and Vegetable Provençale, Saffron Mussels, Yellow Pepper Cream, Baked Beetroot and Parsnip Crisps. (Winner of the *Moreau Chablis Fish Dish of the Year 2003*)
	47	Fillet of Cod with Smoked Salmon, Horseradish, Creamed Leeks, Tomato and Lemon Butter Sauce
	48	Brill in Red Pepper Sauce
	49	Connemara Lobster with Asparagus and Green Beans, Tomato and Garlic Butter
	50-51	Black Sole Fillets, Cauliflower and Spinach Purée, Roasted Vine Tomatoes, Beetroot and Chive Dressing
	52	Connemara Scallops with Butternut Squash Risotto, Timbale of Garlic and Spinach, Chive Beurre Blanc Sauce
Lamb	54	Connemara Lamb with Herb and Mustard Crust, Herb and Apricot Stuffing
	56	Lamb Shanks with Roasted Vegetables
	57	Irish Stew
Chicken	58	Corn-Fed Chicken with Lentils and Wild Mushroom Cream
Beef	59	Fillet Steaks, Puréed Potato, Red Wine and Mushroom Sauce and Béarnaise Sauce
Game	60	Pan-Roasted Quail with Beetroot and Walnut Dressing
	61	Venison with Port and Redcurrant Sauce, Smoked Bacon and Green Cabbage
	62	Crispy Breast of Duckling, Toasted Aubergine, Root Vegetables, Sweet Chilli Sauce and Crispy Green Cabbage
	64	Pheasant with Smoked Bacon and Chestnuts
Vegetarian	66	Leek and Shallot Tart
	67	Aubergine and Tomato Lasagne

DESSERTS

71 Pear and Apricot Filo Roulade

72 Rhubarb and Ginger Crumble with Pistachio Ice Cream

74 Passion-fruit and Vanilla Crème Brulée

76 Chocolate Steamed Puddings

79 Dark and White Chocolate Mousse

80 Dark Chocolate Mousse

81 Bread and Butter Pudding

BREADS, CAKES AND SCONES

Yeast 84

Brown Soda 85

Oatmeal and Buttermilk 85

Fruit Scones 87

Ginger Cake 87

STOCKS

Chicken 90

Vegetable 90

Fish 90

Beef or Veal 91

Lamb 91

SAUCES

Tomato 92

Hollandaise 92

Béarnaise 93

Paloise 93

Mousseline 93

Mayonnaise 93

Salsa Verde 94

Aïoli 94

Honey Dressing 95

Vinaigrette 95

Tomato Fondue 96

Mango, Chilli and Pepper Salsa 96

Basil Oil 97

Basil Pesto 97

Onion Marmalade 98

Mrs Coyle's Crabapple Jelly 99

SIDE DISHES

Herb Crust 100

Couscous 100

Fresh Pasta 101

Puy Lentils 101

Polenta Cake with Herbs 102

Confit of Garlic 103

Garlic Mash 103

Parsnip and Honey Bake 105

Courgettes with Almonds 105

Carrots with Mint, Lemon and
Garlic 106

Basil Mash 106

Puréed Potatoes 107

SWEET SAUCES

Crème Patissière 107

Crème Anglaise 108

Coffee Crème Anglaise 108

Liqueur Crème Anglaise 108

Passion-fruit Sauce 109

Stock Syrup 109

CHRISTMAS AT RENVYLE

Traditional Roast Turkey 113

Roast Goose 114

Apricot, Thyme and Parsley
Stuffing 115

Port & Cranberry Sauce 115

Baked Ham with Cider
and Cloves 116

Brussels Sprouts with Smoked
Bacon 116

Roast Vegetables in a Parcel 117

Mince Pies 119

Christmas Pudding 120

Brandy Sauce 121

Connemara Mussels with Lemongrass and Ginger

This recipe is mostly about assembling chopped vegetables and flavourings and takes no more than 10 minutes to cook. The vegetables can be cooked an hour ahead and the mussels added just before serving. Perfect for a quick supper, starter or lunch with crusty bread.

3 tbsp olive oil
2 cloves garlic, chopped
2 shallots, diced
2 stalks lemongrass, chopped
2 sprigs thyme
50g leeks, chopped
50g carrot, shredded
25g ginger, chopped
15 mussels, washed
150ml cream
150g coconut milk
100ml white wine
2 teaspoons coriander, chopped
Salt & pepper to taste

Heat the oil in a pot; add garlic, leeks, carrots, shallots, ginger and lemongrass. Allow to cook for 4-5 minutes.

Add thyme and keep warm over low heat.

In a separate pot heat wine, add mussels and cook for 3–4 minutes until they open. Discard any mussels that do not open. Remove the mussels and place in a serving dish.

Add the vegetables to the wine and mussel liquid and reduce by one third.

Add the coconut milk and cream and simmer for 3-4 minutes. Season to taste and add coriander. Pour sauce over mussels and serve.

Angel Hair Pasta with Killary Bay Prawns

150g angel hair pasta
3 tbsp olive oil
1 clove garlic, crushed
2 shallots, diced
50g tomatoes, chopped
2 teaspoons tomato purée
300ml double cream
8 prawn tails, raw, shells on
Salt & black pepper to season
4 basil leaves
25g Parmesan, grated

While Killary Bay prawns are served in Renvyle, any plump prawns will do. Make sure frozen prawns are well thawed before cooking. The delicacy of the fine pasta means that the sauce is not overpowered and the sweet flavour of the prawns comes through perfectly. Tinned or fresh tomatoes may be used, depending on the season; tinned are best used in winter. Skin fresh tomatoes by plunging into hot water for a minute.

Remove prawn tails from shells and set aside.

Cook pasta in boiling, salted water for 6 minutes. Drain, refresh in cold water and drain again.
Heat some oil in a pan, add garlic, prawn shells and shallots and cook for 2-3 minutes.

Add tomato purée and simmer for 1 minute, add cream and reduce by a third. Pass the sauce through a fine sieve and season.
Heat remaining oil in a pan, add the prawns and cook for 2 minutes.

Mix in the pasta, diced tomatoes, basil leaves and sauce.

Season with salt and black pepper.

Serve with grated Parmesan.

Tower of Crabmeat, Mixed Salad Leaves, Mango and Spring Onion Salsa

The contrasting tastes here are fresh and appetising for a lunch main course as well as starter. For more simple presentation, substitute won ton sheets with thinly sliced toasted bread or Melba toast. The mango salsa is good with curries and pork dishes.

400g crabmeat
1 sweet apple, diced
1 spring onion, finely chopped
1 lemon zest & juice
1 lime zest & juice

Mix all together and store in the fridge for 4 hours

4 won ton pastry sheets:
Deep fry in oil until crispy

Mango Salsa
1 mango, diced
1 spring onion, diced
Half small red onion, finely chopped
Half chilli, finely chopped
1 tablespoon white wine vinegar
2 tablespoons water
1 tablespoon sugar

In a pot, simmer vinegar, water, sugar and chilli for 4 minutes. Chill and add the mango and spring onion.

Garnish: Mixed salad leaves
Flat leaf parsley

To assemble: Place a mound of crabmeat on the centre of the plate and place won ton on top. Pour salsa around the crab. Place salad leaves around the edge of the plate. Drizzle salad leaves with olive oil.

Garlic Baguette with Serrano Ham and Red Peppers

Serves 4

Good quality Serrrano, Iberico and Prosciutto dried hams are now widely available and are useful storecupboard ingredients. This open sandwich brings together the best of Spanish flavours.

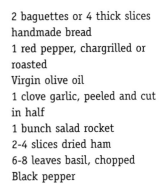

2 baguettes or 4 thick slices handmade bread
1 red pepper, chargrilled or roasted
Virgin olive oil
1 clove garlic, peeled and cut in half
1 bunch salad rocket
2-4 slices dried ham
6-8 leaves basil, chopped
Black pepper

Slice the baguette in half and chargrill until crisp.

Rub with the garlic and olive oil. Layer with peppers, rocket and ham.

Season with black pepper and garnish with basil.

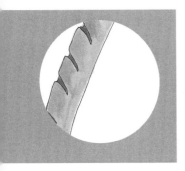

Chicken Mousse with Tarragon

This light mousse can be prepared hours in advance and is useful for parties. Tarragon is an aromatic herb which is best only used fresh. Oregano is a good substitute in this recipe.

100g chicken breast
1 medium egg white
150ml double cream
50g tarragon, chopped
Salt & freshly ground black pepper to season

Pre-heat oven to 190°c/375f/ Gas 5.

Skin the chicken breasts, and cut flesh into small cubes.

Place in a food processor with tarragon and egg white and process to a purée.

Add cream and purée for 1 minute and season with salt and black pepper. Chill for one hour.

Butter four ramekin dishes or ovenproof cups and fill with chicken mousse.

Place in a roasting tray, filling the tray with hot water up to half way of the ramekins. Cover with tin foil and cook for 35 minutes.

Remove from oven and leave to chill.

Serve with a crisp green salad and tomato chutney.

Chicken Liver Paté

Tim's addition of chopped apple,
ginger and redcurrant gives an
added dimension to this smooth
paté, the smoked bacon providing
a rich contrast to their sweetness.

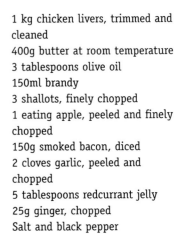

1 kg chicken livers, trimmed and
cleaned
400g butter at room temperature
3 tablespoons olive oil
150ml brandy
3 shallots, finely chopped
1 eating apple, peeled and finely
chopped
150g smoked bacon, diced
2 cloves garlic, peeled and
chopped
5 tablespoons redcurrant jelly
25g ginger, chopped
Salt and black pepper

Heat a large pan, add the oil,
shallots and garlic. Cook for 2-3
minutes.

Add the livers, bacon, apple and
butter and cook for 4-5 minutes.

Add the brandy, redcurrant jelly
and ginger.

Cook for one minute, season with
salt and pepper.

Transfer to a food processor and
blend to a smooth paste.

Line a loaf tin with cling film.
Pour in the paté, cool and place in
the fridge.

Serve with mixed salad leaves and
a fruit chutney.

Mozzarella and Grilled Tomato Salad

The tomatoes can be grilled ahead of time and the salad assembled at the last minute. Grilling the tomatoes brings out their sweetness and combines deliciously with the cheese.

2 tablespoons olive oil
1 garlic clove, crushed
Grated rind 1 lemon
2 teaspoons chopped fresh thyme
8 tomatoes
175g Mozzarella cheese, preferably buffalo
8 large tinned anchovies
2 Little Gem lettuce

Dressing:
6 tablespoons olive oil
1 tablespoon balsamic vinegar
Salt & pepper to taste
4 basil leaves

Place oil in a small bowl with the garlic, lemon rind and thyme. Set aside to infuse for several hours.

Halve the tomatoes lengthwise and carefully scoop out the seeds. Place, cut side down, on a foil-lined grill pan. Brush with a little of the oil mixture and cook under a pre-heated grill, as close to the heat as possible for 3 minutes without charring.

Turn the tomatoes over, drizzle the remaining oil and cook for a further 2-3 minutes. Set aside to chill.

Cut the mozzarella into thin slices. Wash and dry the anchovies and cut into thin strips.
Wash and separate the lettuce leaves and place in a large bowl.

Combine the dressing ingredients until well blended (shake in a screw-topped jar). Pour 2 tablespoons over the lettuce leaves with the basil.

Arrange the lettuce on serving plates, top with the tomatoes, mozzarella and anchovies. Pour over the remaining dressing. Serve at once.

Springroll of Duck and Spicy Stir-Fried Vegetables, with Pineapple and Spring Onion Salsa and Savoury Couscous

The contrast of the duck with the salsa, punctuated with sweet pineapple is perfect and makes a delicious light supper dish as well as a starter. With crusty bread, it is good for lunch too.

2 duck legs
4 tablespoons bean sprouts
Half aubergine, finely sliced
30g green cabbage, shredded
25g ginger, grated
100ml chicken stock
4 sprigs fresh parsley

8 springroll pastry sheets

100g couscous
1 red chilli, diced

Pineapple and Spring Onion Salsa:
Mix together:
Half fresh pineapple, diced
75g spring onion, diced
50g tomato, diced
8 chives, chopped
Juice 2 limes
2 tablespoons olive oil

Heat oven to 200c/240°f/Gas 6 and roast duck legs for 1 hour. Remove skin from duck legs, discard and cut meat into strips. Stir fry vegetables and ginger, add duck meat and leave to cool. Soak couscous with the diced chilli in 100ml of chicken stock until all the stock is absorbed.

Wrap duck and vegetables in pastry, sealing the edges with a little water and shape into rolls.

Cook in hot oil for 3–4 minutes.

Place a ring of couscous on the centre of the plate. Place two springrolls on top. Pour the salsa around the edge of the plate. Garnish with sprigs of parsley.

Goat's Cheese with Rocket and Red Pepper Salsa

Try this dish for lunch or as a substantial starter. The salsa can be prepared a day in advance. Rocket leaves make an interesting peppery contrast to the creamy cheese.

2 small red peppers
6 tablespoons olive oil
1 small red onion
1 garlic clove, peeled
2 tomatoes
30ml balsamic vinegar
Pinch sugar
30g fresh chervil, chopped
Salt & pepper
125g goat's cheese
125g rocket leaves
2 tablespoons pine nuts

Pre-heat oven to 200°c/400f/Gas 6.

Brush the peppers with a little oil and place in a roasting tin. Roast in oven for 30 minutes until charred, turning once.

Transfer to a bowl, cover with a tea-towel and set aside until cool enough to handle.

Carefully peel the peppers over the bowl to catch the juices, then discard the seeds. Chop flesh and add to its juices.

Finely chop the onion and garlic. Immerse the tomatoes in boiling water for 30 seconds, then remove and peel away the skins. Halve, de-seed and dice.

Heat 1 tablespoon of oil in a small pan, add the onion and garlic and fry for about 3 minutes until softened. Add the diced tomatoes and fry gently for a further 2 minutes and add to the peppers, toss to mix and set aside to cool.

Combine the remaining oil with the vinegar, sugar, chervil and seasoning. Drizzle over the pepper mixture.

Slice the goat's cheese.

Divide the rocket between individual plates and arrange the cheese in the centre. Spoon some of the salsa over the cheese and drizzle the rest liberally over the rocket. Scatter with pine nuts.

Renvyle Salad with Smoked Tuna

Smoked tuna is a delicacy produced by excellent smokers in Ireland. Fresh tuna may also be used. This is a substantial salad, ideal for summer suppers and lunches. The anchovies lighten the fish, the new potatoes and French beans combining perfectly with the herbs for a mouthful of varied textures and flavours.

225g small new potatoes
125g French beans
2 eggs, medium
225g fresh smoked tuna
6 tablespoons extra virgin olive oil
3 ripe tomatoes
1 garlic clove, crushed
25g anchovies in oil, drained
25g capers, drained & washed
1 tablespoon red wine vinegar
3 tablespoons fresh basil, chopped
1 tablespoon fresh parsley, chopped
50g black pitted olives
Salt & pepper to season
1 lemon cut into wedges
4 sprigs parsley

Cook the potatoes in lightly salted boiling water for 7-9 minutes till cooked.

Add the beans and cook for a further 3-4 minutes until just tender. Drain and slice the potatoes and place in a large bowl.

Hard boil the eggs for 7–9 minutes. Immediately plunge the eggs into cold water, peel and immerse in fresh cold water until required.

Cut the tuna in strips and add to the potatoes.

Heat oil in a pan. Roughly chop the tomatoes and add to the pan with the garlic, anchovies and capers. Stir fry for 1 minute, then add the remaining oil, vinegar and herbs.

Add to the potato and tuna mixture and toss well.

Divide the salad between individual plates. Cut the eggs into quarters and add to the salad with the olives. Garnish with lemon wedges and parsley and serve.

Connemara Smoked Fish Platter

Nothing in this recipe has to be cooked, it is a job of chopping, grating and assembling good quality ingredients, using a careful balance of flavours.

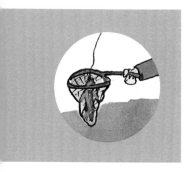

225g raw beetroot
1 garlic clove, crushed
1 tablespoon raspberry red wine vinegar
Pinch sugar
3 tablespoons walnut oil
1 tablespoon extra virgin olive oil
2 tablespoons chopped fresh chives
Salt and pepper
1 smoked trout fillet, skinned
100g smoked tuna
125g smoked salmon
8 slices of wholemeal brown bread
1 lemon cut in wedges

Dressing:
100ml soured cream
2 tablespoons natural yoghurt
1 tablespoon orange juice
15g fresh horseradish root
3 spring onions, trimmed
1 tablespoon fresh dill and chives, chopped

Peel the beetroot, then grate (easiest using a food processor); transfer to a bowl. Add the garlic and toss.

In a small bowl, blend together the vinegar, sugar, walnut oil and olive oil, chives and seasoning. Pour over the beetroot and toss until evenly combined. Cover and leave for 30 minutes to allow the flavours to infuse.

Meanwhile, prepare the dressing. Put the cream, yoghurt and orange juice in a bowl.

Scrub the horseradish, then peel and finely dice; add to the dressing.

Finely chop the spring onions and add to the dressing with the dill and seasoning to taste. Set aside until required.

Arrange the smoked fish and beetroot on individual serving plates. Spoon the horseradish dressing next to the fish and garnish with dill and chives.

Serve with lemon wedges and homemade brown bread.

West Coast Crab Cakes with Coriander, Coconut and Curry Cream

A good balance of crabmeat with herbs and cream means the texture and delicate flavour of the crabmeat is allowed to sing in these crab cakes. The sauce provides a contrasting, subtle and unique pairing and is also useful for serving with fried or steamed fish for a change.

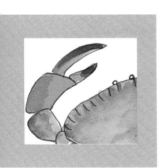

Crab Cake Mix:
340g white crabmeat
2 tablespoons chopped parsley
Zest and juice 1 lemon
2 tablespoons chopped coriander
20ml double cream
2 egg yolks
60g white breadcrumbs
Salt and pepper

Flake the crabmeat into a bowl. Mix with the remaining ingredients and season well.
Roll the mixture into small croquettes and chill for 4-6 hours

Coconut and Curry Cream Sauce:
3 tablespoons olive oil
50g lemongrass
2 cloves garlic, crushed
4 shallots, diced
1 tablespoon ginger, grated
4 sprigs thyme
50g butter
4 tablespoons curry powder
2 tablespoons turmeric
1 litre chicken stock
450ml double cream
240ml coconut milk
Salt and pepper
To garnish: 2 tablespoons chopped chives

Put oil in a large pot over a low heat. Add the shallots, ginger, lemongrass, garlic and thyme and allow to cook slowly with lid on for 3-4 minutes.
Add butter, curry powder, turmeric, chicken stock and cream and bring to the boil.
Simmer for 10 minutes then add coconut milk and cream. Simmer for a further 2-3 minutes.
Pass through a fine sieve and keep warm.

Heat oil in a deep fat fryer to 180°c/350°f. Deep fry the crab cakes until golden brown. Drain on kitchen paper.

To serve: Warm 4 serving plates. Place crab cakes in the middle and pour the sauce around the base of the plate and garnish with chopped chives.

Roulade of the Sea with Cream Cheese, Mixed Salad Leaves and Curried Crème Fraîche

Smoked fish and cream cheese is a perfect classic blend of flavours, with additional contrast provided by the fresh herbs which make an attractive and impressive finish to the roll.

150g smoked salmon, thinly sliced
200g cream cheese
Salt, pepper and lemon juice

Herb Crust:
Use fresh herbs only
200g parsley
200g tarragon
200g fennel
200g chives
1 teaspoon peppercorns

6 prawn tails, cooked, shelled and diced
1 cup crème fraîche
1 teaspoon curry powder
12 washed mixed salad leaves sprinkled with olive oil
1 tomato, finely diced

Finely chop the herbs; season with salt and pepper. Lay 30cm cling film on a work top and cover with the herb crust mix.

Put the cream cheese in a bowl and mix in the prawns and lemon juice.

Place the smoked salmon on top of the herbs. Cover with the cheese mix and roll into a roulade. Chill in the fridge for 4-5 hours.

Mix the curry powder into the crème fraîche.

To serve: Slice the roulade in 5cm rolls. Place in the centre of the plate. Garnish with curry crème fraîche, diced tomato and mixed salad leaves.

Oyster Soup

This is an easy soup with a touch of luxury and has a taste of the sea with a little more depth than when eaten from the shell. The Tabasco gives it a lift too and fresh fennel finishes it perfectly.

600ml fish stock (see p.90)
300ml cream
150ml dry white wine
4 drops Tabasco
12 oysters
Garnish: 1 tablespoon fresh chopped fennel

Bring fish stock, cream and wine to the boil and simmer for three minutes. Add oysters and remove from heat.
Liquidise all ingredients in a blender and pour back into pot once more to simmer again. Garnish with chopped fennel.

To open an oyster, only the point of the knife is used (you need to use an oyster knife). Place the oyster in the palm of your hand, push the point of the knife about a half inch deep into the hinge (the pointed side of the oyster) between the lid and body of the oyster. Once the lid has been penetrated, it should open.

Lift up the top shell, cutting the muscle attached to it and remove from shell.

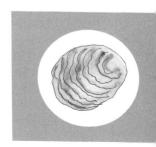

Mushroom Soup

This soup uses potato to thicken it and provide extra flavour. A rich home-made chicken stock is well worth the trouble of boiling the bones from a leftover roasted carcass. Any type of mushroom will do and a mixture of a few exotic ones – shiitake, cepes or chanterelles – added, makes it even more interesting. It can be made a day before serving, up to adding the cream.

40g butter
3 large potatoes, diced
250g mushrooms, chopped
2 medium onions, diced
600ml chicken stock (see p.90)
300ml cream
25g fresh chopped parsley
Salt & pepper to season

Melt butter in a large pot. Add potatoes, mushrooms and onions and cook for 4–5 minutes.

Add chicken stock and bring to the boil.

Add cream and simmer for 10–20 minutes.

Add parsley and blend until smooth or pass through a sieve. Reheat gently, season to taste and serve with some chopped parsley.

Cauliflower and Almond Soup

A powerful combination of tastes, this soup is more unusual than it reads, with great texture contrasts. Perfect for winter lunches - children love it!

75g chopped almonds
75g butter
2 medium onions, chopped
1 head cauliflower, sliced
Pinch saffron strands
1.2 litres chicken stock
Pinch nutmeg
25g flaked almonds, toasted
300ml cream
Salt & pepper to season

Place the chopped almonds on a non-stick pan or toast for two to three minutes in the oven or under the grill.

Melt the butter in a large pot. Add the onions, chopped almonds and cauliflower, cook for 5-8 minutes.

Add the saffron and chicken stock. Bring to the boil and simmer for 20 minutes.

Allow to cool and then purée in a blender

Add the nutmeg.

Return to the pot, heat and add the cream. Season to taste.

Garnish with flaked almonds and cream.

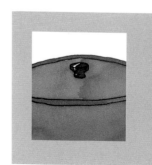

Apple and Onion Soup

Tim's unusual combination of flavours works very well and as the apple and onion season come together is a great way of using windfalls of any type of apple – sweet or cooking varieties. Yoghurt can be used to finish instead of cream.

6 onions, peeled and chopped finely
4 Granny Smith apples, peeled, cored and chopped finely
2 shallots, peeled and chopped finely
110g butter
600ml chicken stock
300ml apple juice
1 tablespoon chopped fresh thyme
3 tablespoons fresh parsley, finely chopped
150ml cream

Melt the butter in a large pot and stir in the apples, shallots and onions for about 5 minutes until soft, but not browned.

Add the stock, parsley, thyme and apple juice; simmer for about 20 minutes.

Cool a little, then whizz in a food processor.

Return to the pot, add the cream and simmer gently for 5 minutes. Do not allow to boil.

Taste for seasoning and serve in warmed soup plates with a sprinkling of the remaining parsley.

Serve with freshly baked brown bread.

Carrot and Orange Soup

A classic flavour blend here
works well, especially when a rich
stock is used. Good with toasted
chunky bread.

30g butter
400g carrots, sliced
400g onions, sliced
1.2 litres chicken stock
1 orange, rind and juice
Salt & pepper to season
Half pint cream

Melt the butter in a large pot, add the
carrots and onions and cook until soft.
Add stock and bring to the boil. Simmer
for 30 minutes.

Allow to cool, then purée in a blender.
Add the juice and orange rind. Return to
the pot and reheat gently. Add cream and
season to taste.

Broccoli and Blue Cheese Soup

Blue cheese, cow or goat, adds a creamy saltiness to the broccoli, while potatoes ensure a grittiness and thick texture. The rosemary flavour comes through gently and the garlic adds depth without over-powering the other ingredients. Two onions may be used instead of one onion and the shallots.

450g broccoli florets
1 large onion, peeled and chopped
3 shallots, peeled and chopped
6 medium potatoes, peeled and diced
50g butter
600ml chicken stock
1 stick celery, finely chopped
1 sprig fresh rosemary, stem removed
1 large clove garlic, peeled, crushed, chopped
Handful parsley, finely chopped
50g blue cheese, diced small
150ml cream

Melt butter and soften the onion and shallot in a large pot.

Add broccoli, potatoes, garlic and rosemary. Cook for 5 minutes. Add celery and stock and simmer for 20 minutes.

Whizz in a food processor. Return to the pot, add the blue cheese, cream and half the parsley, reheating gently without boiling.

Taste for seasoning and serve in warmed soup plates with a sprinkling of the remaining parsley.

Freshly baked brown bread is a perfect accompaniment.

Seafood Chowder

Serves 4-6

Tim is famous for his chowder, made from local fresh fish. The fish stock recipe on p.90 makes for a deliciously rich soup. Don't overdo the smoked haddock as the smoked taste can overpower the fresh. Tim suggests no more than 100g.

50g butter
2 medium onions, diced
50g carrot, diced
50g leeks, diced
50g celery, diced
250g potatoes
300g raw fish, cubed – smoked haddock, cod, shrimp, mussels, salmon, monkfish
Salt and pepper to season
2 bay leaves
125ml cream
600ml fish stock
70ml brandy
50g fresh parsley, chopped

Melt the butter in a large pot. Add carrots, leeks, celery and onion and cook for 3-4 minutes.

Add potatoes, bay leaves and brandy and cook for a further 3 minutes.

Add fish stock and bring to the boil.

Add the fish and simmer for 5-8 minutes over a medium heat.

Add cream and parsley, season with salt and pepper and bring back to the boil.

Serve with wholemeal brown bread.

Asparagus Soup

There is no substitute for fresh asparagus for this recipe, the way that Tim makes it. However, some jars of white asparagus from Spain are good enough for the amateur cook. 2 medium onions instead of the onion and shallots may also be used. Fresh herbs are essential.

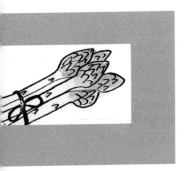

600g fresh asparagus, peeled and diced
1 large onion, diced
2 shallots, diced
100g butter
600ml chicken stock
300ml cream
1 tablespoon chopped fresh thyme
1 tablespoon fresh parsley, chopped

Melt the butter in a pot. Add asparagus, shallots and onions and cook for a few minutes until soft, stirring gently.

Add chicken stock and thyme, bring to the boil and simmer for 5-6 minutes.

Add cream and cook gently for a further 3 minutes.

Blend in a food processor. Garnish with chopped parsley.

Pan-Seared Sea Bass, Basil and Vegetable Provençale,
Saffron Mussels, Yellow Pepper Cream, Baked Beetroot
and Parsnip Crisps.

Serves 2

This dish was National Winner of the *Moreau Chablis Fish Dish of the Year 2003*, and not surprisingly is quite complex with lots of accompaniments to make it so special. Tim goes to a lot of trouble for his diners, but all parts are not difficult for the amateur cook. The Provençale and beetroot can be cooked ahead, but the cream sauce and mussels are best cooked at the last minute. The parsnip crisps can be cooked a few hours ahead.

sea bass

1 whole sea bass (800g)
Heat oven to 200c/400f/Gas 6.
De-scale the sea bass and fillet, remove pin bones and cut into four pieces.
Heat olive oil in a non-stick pan.
Cook fish skin down for 2 minutes.
Transfer to oven for 2 minutes.
Serve with sprigs fresh parsley.

basil & vegetable provencale

50g courgette, diced
50g aubergine, diced
50g fresh tomato, diced
50g onion, diced
50g red pepper, diced
25g tomato purée
1 garlic clove, chopped
Olive oil
Half glass white wine
Salt & pepper to season
4 large basil leaves

Heat oil in the pan, add garlic and vegetables. Cook for 2 minutes.
Add tomato purée and white wine. Cook for a further 1-2 minutes.
Add basil and season with salt and pepper. Keep warm.

yellow pepper cream

2 yellow peppers, diced
1 small onion, diced
25g small leek, diced
1 celery stick, diced
1 clove garlic, chopped
1 sprig thyme, de-stemmed
Salt & pepper
200ml double cream
2 tablespoons olive oil

Heat oil in a pan over moderate
heat, add vegetables, garlic and
thyme. Cook until soft.
Season, add cream and simmer
for 2 minutes.
Blend in a processor and pass
through a fine sieve. Keep warm.

baked beetroot

1 whole beetroot, peeled
1 tablespoon balsamic vinegar
Olive oil
1 teaspoon brown sugar

Cook beetroot in salted water for
20 minutes. Cut beetroot into thin
slices. Pan fry in a skim of olive
oil for 2 minutes. Add vinegar
and sugar and place in oven for
4 minutes.

parsnip crisps

1 parsnip
Peel off the outer skin and with
a vegetable peeler, shave the
parsnip into strips.

Deep fry until golden brown and
crisp. Drain on kitchen paper,
season with salt to taste.

saffron mussels

12 mussels, washed
25g medium onion, diced
1 pinch saffron
25g butter
1 glass white wine
200ml double cream
1 clove garlic, chopped

Scrub the mussels in cold water,
pulling off beard as much as
possible.

Put in a pot with onion, half the
wine, the parsley and garlic. Cook
until mussels open, discarding any
that don't.

Remove flesh from shells.
Add remaining wine, cream and
saffron to pot and reduce by 1/2
and whisk in the butter. Add
mussels and keep warm.

to serve

Place a round mould in the centre
of the plate and fill with the
Vegetable Provencale. Place mussels near base of vegetables. Pour
yellow pepper cream around the
base of plate with beetroot.

Remove the mould and place fish
on top of vegetables, topping with
parsnip crisps. Garnish with whole
flat leaf parsley.

Fillet of Cod with Smoked Salmon, Horseradish, Creamed Leeks, Tomato and Lemon Butter Sauce.

This shows one of Tim's strengths where unusual flavours are married to amazing effect. The horseradish sauce strengthens the cod flavour while contrasting with the oiliness of the smoked salmon; the lemon butter sauce is soft and creamy with a citrus kick.

600g fresh fillet cod, bones removed
4 slices smoked salmon
4 dessertspoons horseradish sauce
Teaspoon dill, chopped
50g sesame seeds
Juice half lemon
100ml cream
50g butter
35ml olive oil
Salt & pepper to season

Tomato and Lemon Butter Sauce:
3 shallots, chopped
2 fresh tomatoes, skinned & diced
20ml white wine vinegar
20ml white wine

100g butter
100ml cream
Juice half lemon

In a heavy saucepan place shallots, vinegar and wine, cook for 3-4 minutes.
Add cream, bring to the boil, remove from heat.
Whisk in butter, add the diced tomato, lemon juice and season to taste.
Keep warm over a gentle heat.

Fish:
Heat oven to 200c/400f/Gas 6.
Season with salt, pepper and lemon juice. Coat the fish with horseradish, place smoked salmon on top and sprinkle with dill and sesame seeds.
Heat a hot griddle pan, add some olive oil and seal the base of the fish for 1 minute.
Transfer to oven and cook for 10 minutes.

Leeks: Pan fry the leeks in butter add cream, season to taste.

To serve: Divide leeks between 4 warm plates, remove fish from oven and place on top of leeks. Garnish with the tomato and lemon butter sauce.

Brill in Red Pepper Sauce

Not all fish is suited to the flavour of red pepper, but brill is a good example of it working well, especially with spinach as an accompaniment.

4 x 150g fillets brill
2 large red peppers, roughly chopped
25g small onion, roughly chopped
2 small garlic cloves, peeled and crushed
1 litre fish stock See p.90
2 sprigs thyme
Squeeze fresh lemon juice
400g spinach leaves
40ml olive oil

Heat a medium size pot with a little oil, add onions and cook for 2–3 minutes.

Add garlic, thyme and peppers and cook for a further 2 minutes. Add stock, cover and simmer for 12 minutes.

Liquidise, taste and season. Strain and keep hot.

Pan-fry the spinach in oil with the garlic.

Season brill fillets and sprinkle with lemon juice. Grill for 5 minutes.

Serve the brill with the pepper sauce and spinach.

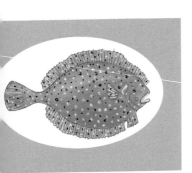

Connemara Lobster, with Asparagus and Green Beans, Tomato and Garlic Butter

Lobster is a treat wherever it is caught and the flavour of Connemara lobster is superb. Tim makes the best of it by serving it with light flavours which allow the sweetness of the lobster to speak for itself.

Lobster:
2 litres salted water
4 x 960g lobsters

In a large pot bring the salted water to the boil. Add the whole lobsters and simmer for 10-12 minutes. Remove the lobsters and keep warm.

When ready to serve, split the lobsters in half and remove the heads, leaving the meat in the tails. Remove the meat from the claws by crushing the shells.

Asparagus and green beans:
100g French beans, topped and tailed
100g asparagus, washed and peeled.

Bring a small pot of salted water to the boil and cook the beans and asparagus for 3 minutes, then drain and keep warm.

Tomato and Garlic Butter:
2 shallots, diced
2 fresh tomatoes, diced
2 cloves garlic, chopped
1 handful parsley, chopped
100g butter
20ml olive oil
Salt and pepper
Juice half lemon

Heat a pan and add oil, shallots and garlic and cook for 2-3 minutes, add butter, tomato, parsley and lemon juice. Simmer for 2 minutes.

To serve:
Heat four serving plates. Place the vegetables on the centre, sit the lobster tails and claws on top. Pour over the tomato and garlic butter. Grill for 1 minute. Sprinkle over some parsley on top when ready to serve.

Black Sole Fillets, Cauliflower and Spinach Purée, Roasted Vine Tomatoes, Beetroot and Chive Dressing

Chef Tim tends to be generous in his portions and often serves three fillets per person. We are allowing two each here. It's well worthwhile cooking all the elements of this dish to get a superb combination of tastes and textures. Nothing is complicated, and the beetroot and chive dressing can be made well in advance.

Fish:
8 black sole fillets
Salt & pepper

Cook this last when everything else has been prepared.
Heat 1 tablespoon oil in a pan.
Cook seasoned sole fillets for 2-3 minutes on each side.

Cauliflower purée:
2 heads cauliflower, diced
100ml cream
12 spinach leaves
1 tablespoon olive oil

Place cauliflower in a large pot with cream. Cook until tender – 15–20 minutes.
Fry spinach leaves in oil.
Blend all in a food processor.
Keep warm.

Roast tomatoes:
4 fresh tomatoes
Olive oil
Sea salt

Cut tomatoes in half, scoop out the flesh. Place on a roasting tray with olive oil and sea salt.
Bake in a low oven for 6 hours, 150°c/300°f/Gas 2.
This is best done the night before.

Beetroot and Chive Dressing:
1 shallot, diced
1 glass white wine
Half glass white wine vinegar
50ml cream
100g butter
1 beetroot, cooked and diced
1 cup chopped chives
Salt and pepper to season

Place shallot, white wine and wine vinegar in a pot and reduce by half.

Add cream and bring to the boil. Remove from heat and whisk in butter.

Add diced beetroot and chives. Keep warm.

To serve:
Place cauliflower and spinach purée in the centre of each plate.

Pour the beetroot and chive dressing around the rest of the plate. Sit the sole fillets on the purée.

Garnish with roasted tomatoes and some whole chives.

Connemara Scallops with Butternut Squash Risotto, Timbale of Garlic Spinach and Chive Beurre Blanc Sauce

The delicacy of scallops is carefully protected by the careful judging of the squash in the risotto and the lightness of the spinach served with a rich, but delicate, buttery sauce. Risotto is a serious dish and cannot be left to cook by itself, requiring the addition of the stock a little at a time. This is quite a complex dish and is best finished while diners are seated and enjoying the aromas as you cook.

Butternut squash purée:
2 butternut squash
4 tablespoons olive oil
2 shallots, diced
80ml cream
300ml vegetable stock
Peel and cut squash into cubes.
Heat olive oil in a pot and gently cook diced shallots for 2-3 minutes.

Add squash and cook for 10 minutes.
Add cream and vegetable stock and cook until soft.
Purée in a blender. Keep warm.

Risotto:
150g arborio or carnaroli rice
5 tablespoons olive oil
75g butter
2 shallots, diced
1 garlic clove, crushed
600ml vegetable stock (p.90)

Heat oil and butter in a large pot. Add shallots and garlic and cook for 3 minutes until soft.

Add rice and stir well to coat all grains.

Add stock a little at a time, continuously stirring until the liquid is absorbed. The rice will be cooked when it feels tender.

Mix the squash purée with the rice.

Chive Beurre Blanc Sauce:
1 shallot, diced
Half glass white wine
3 tablespoons white wine vinegar
80ml cream
75g butter
50g chives, chopped

In a small pot cook the shallots, white wine and white wine vinegar. Reduce by half.
Add cream and bring to the boil. Remove from the heat and whisk in butter and chives.

Spinach:
350g fresh spinach leaves
Skim olive oil
Cook the spinach in 1 tablespoon oil with garlic and cream for 2-3 minutes.

Scallops:
15 scallops
Olive oil
Heat a light coating of oil in a hot pan and add scallops. Cook for 2-3 minutes on either side. Place on kitchen paper and keep warm.

To serve: Place a medium size pastry cutter on the centre of the plate and fill tightly with risotto. Place a smaller ring on top and fill with spinach. Pour sauce on the base of the plate. Place scallops around the plate. Remove pastry cutters and garnish with chopped chives.

Connemara Lamb with Herb and Mustard Crust, Herb and Apricot Stuffing, Ratatouille and Rosemary Gravy

Connemara lamb is known worldwide for its sweetness, tenderness and a hint of wild herbs. Tim's recipe is not difficult, but the lamb needs to be watched so it is not over-done. His stuffing is delicious and moist; the other accompaniments are optional. Traditional, simple roast potatoes, peas, and carrots work well too.

2 racks lamb, trimmed
Salt & pepper to taste
Rosemary
2 teaspoons Dijon mustard
1 teaspoon mixed fresh herbs – parsley, thyme, mint
1 dessertspoon breadcrumbs

Heat oven to 200°c/400°f/Gas 6.
Heat a large griddle pan and season the lamb with salt and pepper.
Seal the lamb on both sides, add a little rosemary and place in a roasting tin in a fairly hot oven for 18 minutes or until cooked as you like it.

To finish the lamb: Coat the outside surface with a mixture of mustard, the remaining crumbs and the herbs. Finish under a hot grill for 2 minutes to crisp and brown.

Herb & Apricot Stuffing
75-100g butter
2 shallots, diced
75g mixed fresh herbs – parsley, thyme, mint
50g dried apricots, chopped
100g fresh white breadcrumbs
To make stuffing: Melt the butter in a pot, add the herbs, chopped apricots and shallots. Cook for about 3 minutes, add the breadcrumbs and keep warm.

Ratatouille:
Half aubergine
1 red pepper, de-seeded
1 courgette
6 mushrooms
1 clove garlic
1 tablespoon olive oil
2 tomatoes, skinned, de-seeded and chopped
Dice all ingredients finely and cook in oil for 5 minutes.
Keep warm.

Rosemary gravy:
1 glass red wine
Rosemary
1 teaspoon redcurrant jelly
25g butter
Heat a saucepan, add the red wine and chopped rosemary. Reduce by 1/3, add the redcurrant jelly and add in butter a little at a time.

Garnish:
1 parsnip, thinly sliced lengthways
Parsley
Pesto (optional, see p. 97).
Deep fry the sliced parsnips in hot oil until crisp.

To serve: Cut the racks of lamb in half. Place the ratatouille on the centre of the plate and set the lamb on top, garnished with the deep fried parsnips and flat leaf parsley.

Pour the gravy onto the base with the pesto. Place the stuffing beside the ratatouille. Serve immediately with extra seasonal vegetables.

Lamb Shanks with Roasted Vegetables

This economical dish is hearty and full of flavour and butchers are pleased when customers ask for this cut as so many prefer classic, larger leg joints. Tim's secret is long, slow cooking which results in meat falling off the bone, juicy and tender.

Ingredients
4 lamb shanks
3 tablespoons olive oil
4 sprigs rosemary
Salt and black pepper
20g butter
2 cloves garlic, chopped
2 tablespoons fresh parsley, chopped
150g carrots, cut into small chunks
150g parsnips, cut into small chunks
8 shallots, peeled
Water
Flat leaf parsley

Pre-heat oven to 170°c/325°f/Gas 3.

Heat oil in a large roasting dish and brown the shanks on all sides. Remove and brown the vegetables. Remove the vegetables and return the shanks and juices to the dish with rosemary and garlic and half a glass of water.

Season with salt and pepper. Cover the dish with tin foil and cook for 90 minutes.

Add the vegetables and continue to cook for a further 30 minutes or until vegetables are tender.

Remove from oven, place the shanks and vegetables on a dish and keep warm.

Strain off the juices into a small pot.

Remove any visible fat from the juice. Boil for 5-6 minutes until it has a light sauce consistency. Remove from the heat and whisk in the butter, then add the chopped parsley and chives.

To serve:
Warm four large plates. Place a shank of lamb in the centre of each. Surround with vegetables and coat with the sauce.

Irish Stew

There is a debate about whether it is traditional to add carrots to lamb stew, but Tim likes to cook all the vegetables together and the result is a flavoursome concoction which would make any Irish person proud. It is a perfect example of a one-pot wonder.

800g shoulder lamb, cubed
220g potatoes, peeled and cut into chunks
200g carrots, thickly sliced
200g small shallots, peeled
120g leeks, sliced
1.5 litres water
3 sprigs thyme
1 large cup parsley leaves
2 tablespoons butter
Salt and black pepper
2 bay leaves
1 clove garlic, chopped

Put the lamb and water in a large pot and bring to the boil, add a little salt and simmer for 30-40 minutes. Strain off any fat from the top.

Add the potatoes and simmer for 25 minutes.

Add the rest of the vegetables, thyme, bay leaves and garlic and simmer for a further 30 minutes.

Add parsley and butter. Cook for a further 2-3 minutes.

Season to taste and serve.

Corn-fed Chicken Breast with Lentils and Wild Mushroom Cream

The blend of lentils with chicken here is French in style and makes it even healthier. Use the best possible chicken breasts for the best flavour. Corn-fed chicken generally has a deeper flavour which is enhanced by Tim's use of wild mushrooms. However, button mushrooms also work well. Parsley can be used instead of coriander and natural yoghurt instead of cream.

4 chicken breasts, skins on
150g lentils
1 litre chicken stock (p.90)
Salt and pepper
Half onion, diced
2 carrots, diced
1 celery stick, diced
40g wild mushrooms, sliced
180ml cream
2 tablespoons olive oil
8 fresh coriander sprigs

Soak the lentils in water overnight. Drain and put into a pot with the stock and a teaspoon of salt. Bring to the boil.

Add the vegetables, cover and simmer for 10-15 minutes. Remove from the heat and keep warm. Season the chicken breasts with salt and pepper.

Heat a heavy frying pan and add oil. Cook chicken breasts over a medium heat for 6-7 minutes on each side.

Remove from the pan and keep warm. Add the mushrooms to the pan and cook for 2 minutes. Add cream and coriander and reduce by one third. Season to taste.

To serve: Warm four serving plates. Place lentils in the middle of each plate. Sit a chicken breast on top and pour the wild mushroom sauce around the base. Garnish with sprigs of coriander.

Fillet Steaks, Puréed Potato, Red Wine and Mushroom Sauce and Béarnaise Sauce

This is a dish that will satisfy meat lovers and those who enjoy a rich sauce with it. Dense reductions of wine and vegetables make this a superbly flavoursome, satisfying dish which is easy to prepare. Button mushrooms can replace Tim's choice of shiitake which have more flavour, but the result is still excellent. Save leftovers from bottles of wine as the amount is reduced by half and will increase in intensity.

4 x 180g trimmed fillet steaks
Season steaks with salt and pepper.
Heat 20g butter in a frying pan. Add steaks and cook for 4 minutes on either side. Transfer to a dish and keep warm.

Red Wine & Mushroom Sauce:
2 shallots, finely diced
30g shiitake mushrooms, sliced
250ml red wine
200ml beef stock (see p.91)
20g butter

Salt and black pepper

Add shallots to the pan in which the steak was cooked and cook for 2 minutes until soft.
Add mushrooms, red wine and stock and reduce by half and whisk in the butter.

450g puréed potato (see p.107)
Béarnaise Sauce (see p.93)
4 sprigs parsley
Parsnip crisps (see p.46)

To assemble: Heat the puréed potato and place in the centre of each of the 4 warmed serving plates. Place the fillets on top. Pour the béarnaise sauce on the beef. Put under a grill for 30 seconds.

Pour the red wine and mushroom sauce around the base of the plate and garnish with parsley and fried parsnip crisps.

Pan-Roasted Quail with Beetroot and Walnut Dressing

Serves 1 person

Quail is now readily available in supermarkets and butchers' shops and has a finer, more delicate flavour than many other game species. The combination of tomatoes, pear and bacon is superb. It makes a delicious lunch or supper dish.

Quail:
1 quail, breast and legs removed
1 teaspoon diced streaky bacon
Salt and pepper

Cook the bacon for 2-3 minutes until crispy. In a non-stick frying pan heat the remaining oil. Season the quail with salt and pepper. Cook for 3–4 minutes.

Dressing:
1 teaspoon red wine vinegar
1 teaspoon maple syrup
2 teaspoons olive oil
15g walnuts
1 small beetroot, cooked & diced

In a bowl, whisk the oil, vinegar and syrup together, add walnuts and beetroot. Chill.
Heat a pan with some olive oil and fry the croutons until golden brown.

To serve:
1 bunch mixed salad leaves
1 teaspoon croutons
1 teaspoon diced pear
1 teaspoon chopped sun-dried tomatoes

Place the leaves on the centre of a warm plate with the croutons, bacon, pear and sun-dried tomatoes. Place the quail on top and sprinkle with the dressing.

Venison with Port and Redcurrant Sauce, Smoked Bacon and Green Cabbage

Widely available, venison is a nutritious and low fat red meat which is redolent of winter. Here, Tim adds an amazing array of flavours which smell as good as they taste. Perfect for a candlelit dinner with a bottle of rich, red wine.

Venison:
1 kg venison fillet
1 teaspoon salt
1 teaspoon black pepper
3 tablespoons oil
30g butter

Trim the venison fillet and cut into 4 portions, season with salt and pepper. Heat the oil and butter in a large pan, add the venison and cook on both sides for 3-4 minutes. Transfer to a serving dish and keep warm.

Smoked Bacon and Cabbage:
1 dessertspoon olive oil
12 leaves green cabbage, finely shredded
40g smoked bacon, diced
Heat olive oil in a pan, cook bacon and cabbage for 4-5 minutes. Keep warm over a low heat.

Port and Redcurrant Sauce:
100ml Port
Zest 1 orange
1 teaspoon fresh grated ginger
125g redcurrants
2 tablespoons redcurrant jelly
Thyme sprigs

Pour port into a saucepan and bring to the boil. Add the orange zest, ginger and redcurrant jelly. Reduce by one third, then add the redcurrants. Bring back to the boil for 2 minutes.

To serve:
Transfer the venison to four warm plates. Pour the sauce around the base and garnish with sprigs of thyme.
Serve with smoked bacon and green cabbage.

Crispy Breast of Duckling, Toasted Aubergine, Root Vegetables, Sweet Chilli Sauce and Crispy Green Cabbage

This unique combination of flavours and textures will be no trouble to any level of cook and yet is a gourmet dish. The vegetables can cook at the same time as the duck breasts – an excellent quick and healthy recipe.

4 duck breasts, skin on
75g green cabbage
4 thin slices aubergine
1 medium egg white
25g sesame seeds
50g parsnips
50g carrots
50g bok choy
50g celeriac
50g baby leeks
Salt and pepper
50g sweet chilli sauce
Half cup cream
50g butter
6g fresh ginger, grated
1 glass olive oil

Salt and black pepper to season

Pre-heat oven to 200°c/400°f/ Gas 6.

Prepare the vegetables first: Peel the vegetables and cut into cubes (except for cabbage and aubergines).

Cook in a pot with the oil and ginger for 10-15 minutes. Season to taste. Keep warm.

In a hot pan heat 1/3 of oil. Season the duck breasts with salt and pepper and seal in the pan on both sides. Place in oven for 10-15 minutes. When cooked keep warm under a grill to crisp the skin.

Shred the cabbage very finely and deep fry in hot oil until crisp for 2–3 minutes until crisp. Place on kitchen paper.

Put the cream in a pot and reduce by half and add the sweet chilli sauce. Season the aubergines, dip in egg white and coat with sesame seeds. Deep fry in hot oil until crisp.

To serve: Place the vegetable mixture on the centre of each warm plate with the aubergine. Place the duck on top with the cabbage, pour sauce on the base of the plate and sprinkle with sweet chilli sauce.

Pheasant with Smoked Bacon and Chestnuts

Pheasant can be quite dry if over-cooked, so watch the timing carefully when roasting. Tim gets over this problem by cooking it in a sauce which keeps it moist and adds a mellow richness.

2 pheasants, oven ready
200g chestnuts, tinned
250g smoked bacon, cubed
25ml vegetable oil
50g butter
4 shallots, diced
40g plain flour
4-5 sprigs thyme
Salt and pepper
400ml beef stock (see p.91)
20ml red wine
Grated rind and juice 1 orange
20ml redcurrant jelly
Chopped parsley to garnish

Preheat oven to 180°c /350°f/ Gas 4.

Heat the oil and butter in a large pan. Add the pheasants and fry until golden brown on all sides. Remove from the pan and place in a casserole dish.

Reheat the pan and fry the chestnuts, bacon and onions for 3-4 minutes. Add to the pheasant. Stir in the flour to the pan and cook for 1 minute.

Add the stock and wine. Bring to the boil until it thickens.

Add orange juice and rind, red currant jelly and thyme and mix well. Pour over the pheasant and place in oven for 1 hour.

Remove from oven and season to taste. Sprinkle with chopped parsley.

Serve with vegetables of your choice – celeriac, turnip and creamed cabbage work well.

Leek and Shallot Tart

Tim recommends Emmenthal for this light tart with a special flavour, but any cheese may be used. Try hard cheeses such as Irish Gabriel or Desmond, Italian Parmesan or aged Spanish Manchego sheep's cheese. Onions can replace leeks when out of season.

Pastry:
220g plain flour
150g butter
1 medium egg yolk
70ml cold water

Mix flour, egg yolk, water, salt and butter in a large bowl.
Knead lightly until firm and chill, wrapped in clingfilm or foil, for 40 minutes.
Roll out the pastry thinly. Cut into the shape of the cake tin and lay it on top, tucking in the edges.

Filling:
375g shallots, peeled & cut in half
1kg leeks, washed & chopped
2 tablespoons olive oil

50g butter
2 tablespoons brown sugar

Salt and pepper to season
140g Emmenthal cheese, grated

Preheat oven to 200°c/400°f/ Gas 6.

Heat a pan with the oil and cook the shallots and leeks until tender. Cool and drain.

Heat a small pan, add butter and sugar. Allow to darken slightly and pour on to the pastry case.
Arrange the leeks and shallots over the sugar mixture.

Season with salt and pepper. Scatter with the grated cheese.

Bake in oven for 25 minutes. When cooked transfer to a warmed plate and serve with a seasonal salad.

Aubergine and Tomato Lasagne

Drain pasta and layer with aubergine mix and Parmesan.

Top with Parmesan shavings and garnish with chopped basil.

This healthy vegetarian dish is easy to make and looks well with its layers of colours. Irish hard cheeses can replace Parmesan.

1 aubergine, cut in thin slices lengthways
220g cherry tomatoes, cut in half
4 tablespoons olive oil
6 sheets lasagne
1 clove garlic, crushed
2 tablespoons tomato purée
80g Parmesan shavings
Salt & black pepper to season
4-6 chopped basil leaves

Brush aubergines and tomatoes with oil. Cook on a heated griddle until charred and tender. Remove and set aside.

Put lasagne sheets in lightly salted water for 2 minutes.

Heat oil in a pan, add garlic and tomato purée, aubergines and tomatoes and cook for 2 minutes. Season.

Pear and Apricot Filo Roulade

Filo pastry is now available in super-markets and is not difficult to use as long as it is kept moist by brushing with melted better. If it dries out, it becomes impossible to use, though it can be cut into squares and baked and served on the side with ice-cream, mousses or with vegetables.

100g fresh apricots, chopped
30ml honey
1 teaspoon lemon juice
50g brown sugar
2 pears, diced
50g ground almonds
25g butter
30g sliced almonds
6 sheets filo pastry
Icing sugar to dust
crème anglaise (see p.108)

Preheat oven to 200°c/400°f/ Gas 6

Lightly grease a baking tray.

Heat the apricots, lemon juice, honey, brown sugar and pears gently for 5 minutes. Allow to cool. Add sliced and ground almonds.

Melt butter. Layer the pastry on the tray brushing each layer with butter. Place the filling down one side of the pastry.

Fold the pastry over the filling, tucking the edge underneath. Seal the ends and brush all over with butter.

Bake for 15-20 minutes, until golden brown.

Remove from oven, slice into four and dust with icing sugar. Serve with crème anglaise.

Rhubarb and Ginger Crumble with Pistachio Ice-Cream

This has wonderful summer flavours and a few levels of crunch with the toasted nuts and topping contrasting with a delicious creamy rhubarb filling.

Ice-cream:
50g pistachio nuts, skinned
3 tablespoons pistachio paste (or pulverized pistachios)
600ml crème anglaise (see p.108)
1 tablespoon icing sugar

Toast the pistachio nuts until brown.
Mix the pistachio paste with the crème anglaise.

When the nuts are cool, add to the mix.
Freeze in a plastic tub.
This is best made 24 hours in advance.

Crumble Filling:
200g rhubarb
100g granulated sugar
25g butter
3 tablespoons maple syrup

Cut rhubarb into cubes and cook gently in a saucepan with the sugar, butter and maple syrup for 10 minutes. Divide between 4 ramekin dishes.

Crumble Topping:
50g plain flour
25g butter
25g brown sugar
25g pistachio nuts, toasted and chopped
Pinch ground ginger

Pre heat oven to 200°c/400f/ Gas 6.

Mix the flour, butter, sugar and pistachios and ginger in a food processor. Pour on top of the rhubarb and bake in a hot oven for 20 minutes.

Serve warm with the ice-cream.

Passion-fruit and Vanilla Crème Brulée

This twist on the classic dish lightens the creamy custard and has a tropical scent.

450ml cream
1 vanilla pod
7 medium egg yolks
100g granulated sugar
120g caster sugar
3 passion-fruit, pulp
4 sprigs mint

Preheat oven to 180°c/350f/Gas 4

Put cream and vanilla pod in a pot and bring to the boil over a medium heat.

Whisk the egg yolks and caster sugar in a large bowl.

When the cream is hot, remove the vanilla pod.

Whisk the cream into the egg mix slowly. Add the seeds from the vanilla pod with the passion-fruit to the mix.

Divide into 6 ramekin dishes. Fill a shallow roasting pan with water to half way. Place dishes in water and bake in oven for 30 minutes. Remove dishes from water and chill for 3-4 hours.

To serve, sprinkle some sugar on top, caramelise with a propane torch or place under hot grill. Garnish with fresh mint leaves.

Chocolate Steamed Puddings

This is not as heavy as puddings often are, the dark chocolate giving it a lift. The filling seeps out when the outside layer is pierced, releasing a rich indulgence. Large cups can be used instead of individual pudding bowls.

Filling:
80ml cream
100g plain chocolate
2 teaspoons brandy

Heat the cream in a pan until hot but not boiling. Remove from heat and add the chocolate. Stir until melted and add the brandy. Pour into a bowl and chill for 2-3 hours.

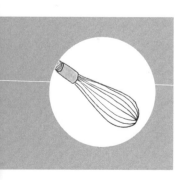

Pudding case:
100g butter, softened
100g caster sugar
2 medium eggs
90g self-raising flour
50g cocoa powder

Preheat oven to 200°c/400°f /Gas 6.

Lightly grease 4 x 150ml pudding moulds. Line the bases with greaseproof paper.

Cream together the butter and sugar in a bowl.

Gradually add the eggs, beating well.

Sift the flour and cocoa powder into the mixture and stir lightly. Spoon 1 tablespoon pudding mixture into the base of each mould. Place a ball of chocolate filling into each mould.

Top the remaining with pudding mixture. Level and cover with greaseproof paper.

Secure with string.

Place moulds on a grill rack over a roasting tin half filled with boiling water.

Cover with foil, place in oven and cook for 30-35 minutes.
Turn the puddings out onto warmed serving plates and dust with icing sugar.

Dark and White Chocolate Mousse

Serves 6

Another recipe for chocolate lovers, this one looks great in glasses as well as traditional ramekins.

200g dark chocolate
120g white chocolate
90g caster sugar
3 medium egg whites
580ml cream
1 tablespoon cocoa powder
6 sprigs mint

Break the chocolate into small pieces. Place the dark chocolate and white chocolate into separate bowls. Melt over pans of simmering water. Remove from heat.

Heat the sugar with 5 tablespoons water to dissolve. Stir two-thirds into the dark chocolate and the remainder into the white. Cool to room temperature.

Whip the cream in a separate bowl.

Whisk the egg whites into soft peaks.

Fold two-thirds of the cream and egg whites into the dark chocolate and fold the remaining cream and egg whites into the white chocolate mixture.

Divide half the dark chocolate mousse into 6 individual ramekin dishes.

Spoon over the white chocolate mousse, followed by the remaining dark chocolate mousse.

Chill for 2-4 hours. Dust the tops with cocoa powder and garnish with sprigs of mint and serve.

Dark Chocolate Mousse

Tim serves this in the restaurant with beautifully crafted shapes, but the home cook can decorate with thin squares. The contrast of the dark, intense chocolate case against the softer filling is indulgence in a small pot.

Mousse:
400g dark chocolate, chopped
25g butter
8 medium eggs, separated
50g castor sugar
1 orange, zest only
70ml orange liqueur
300ml whipping cream
75g white chocolate

Place the dark chocolate and butter in a bowl set over a pan of simmering water and melt, remove from heat.

In another bowl whisk egg yolks, sugar, zest and liqueur. Set the bowl over the simmering water and cook until the mixture becomes very thick, whisking continuously. Remove from heat and fold in the dark chocolate. Cool for 5 minutes.

Whisk the cream and fold into the chocolate mix.

Whisk egg whites until stiff and fold into the chocolate mix.

Chocolate cases:
Melt 75g each of dark and white chocolate in a bowl over boiling water.

Remove and pour onto greaseproof paper.

When cool, cut into 30cm strips and shape into a case.

Place in fridge to set.

Freeze the rest of the chocolate and when hard cut into spheres for decoration.

Fill the chocolate cases with mousse and refrigerate until chilled.

To serve, garnish with chocolate spheres.

Bread and Butter Pudding

Serves 5

This is a traditional Irish dish which has wonderful aromas from the vanilla pod and sweet sultanas.

8 slices white bread
220g unsalted butter, melted
250ml milk
280ml cream
1 vanilla pod, split
6 medium eggs
45g caster sugar
70g sultanas
Pinch salt

Preheat oven to 190°c/375°f/Gas 5

Use a little butter to grease a dish (25cm x 25cm and 5cm deep).

Dip the bread in the butter and place in the dish.

Bring the milk, cream and salt to the boil with the vanilla pod.

Whisk the eggs and sugar and add to the cream and milk mixture.

Pour this custard over the bread and sprinkle the sultanas on top.

Cook in oven for 40-50 minutes in a bain marie roasting dish with simmering water coming half-way up the bowl. This will provide a gentle heat and cook the pudding evenly.

To serve cut into rings using a pastry cutter and serve with hot crème anglaise (p.108).

Yeast Bread

This mix can be used for different varieties of breads adding 20g of rosemary, thyme and onion, tomato and basil, cranberry, apricot and curry powder.

25g fresh yeast
650g strong white flour
20g granulated white sugar
25g butter
12fl oz water
1 teaspoon salt
Sesame seeds

Preheat oven to 230°c/450°f/Gas 8. Dissolve the yeast in 6 fl oz of lukewarm water.

Put the sugar, butter and salt into a bowl with 6fl oz of hot water. Mix until the butter melts. Add to the yeast.

Sieve the flour into a bowl, pour in the liquid and mix.

Place the dough on a floured worktop and leave to relax for 5-6 minutes. Knead until smooth.

Place the dough in a bowl, cover with cling film and wait until it rises to double its size – about 25 minutes.

Knead again for 2-3 minutes and place in a 500g loaf tin.

Cover with a light tea towel and place in a warm area for 30 minutes.

Brush with a little water and sprinkle with sesame seeds.

Bake in oven for 40 minutes.

Remove from the tin and allow to cool.

Brown Soda Bread

250g wholemeal flour
220g white flour
1 teaspoon bread soda
1 teaspoon salt
2 teaspoons baking powder
380ml buttermilk
1 medium egg beaten

Preheat oven to 190°c/375°f/Gas 5.
Sift the flours, bread soda, baking powder
and salt together.

Add the buttermilk and egg and mix lightly.
Knead lightly on a floured surface until
smooth.

Shape into a round and place on a baking
tray. Make a cross shape on top of the cake
and bake in oven for 35–40 minutes until
lightly browned.

Oatmeal and Buttermilk Bread

230g porridge flakes
230g plain white flour
380ml buttermilk
1 teaspoon baking powder
1 teaspoon salt
2 tablespoons granulated sugar

Preheat oven to 200°c/400°f/Gas 6.
In a large bowl mix the porridge flakes, salt,
sugar and milk. Leave to sit for 6-8 hours.

Mix again and add the flour and baking
powder to a fairly stiff dough.

Grease two loaf tins and put in mix.
Bake for 40-45 minutes.

Fruit Scones

400g plain white flour
Half teaspoon salt
100g margarine or butter
4 teaspoons baking powder
300ml milk
90g granulated sugar
120g sultanas
1 medium egg, beaten

Preheat oven to 170°c/325°f/Gas 3.
Sift the flour and salt and lightly rub in the margarine or butter.

Sift in the baking powder and sugar and add the sultanas. Mix well.

Add all the milk and beaten egg and mix to a spongy dough. Knead lightly to make the dough smooth and roll out to half an inch thick.

Cut out with a 5 cm cutter, brush with egg and bake in oven for 10-15 minutes.

Ginger Cake

90g brown sugar
50g butter, heated
2 medium eggs, beaten
3 tablespoons treacle
220g plain flour
Pinch salt
Half teaspoon grated lemon
220ml boiling water
Half teaspoon cinnamon and nutmeg
1 teaspoon ground ginger
4 teaspoons baking powder

Preheat oven to 190°c/375°f/Gas 5.
Beat the sugar and butter in a mixing bowl until light.

Gradually add the egg and treacle, beating after each addition. Add the grated lemon. In another bowl sift together the flour, salt, cinnamon, nutmeg, ginger and baking powder and fold into the egg mixture. Add boiling water, mix well.

Pour into a well greased shallow 1kg baking tin and bake for 40-45 minutes.

STOCKS, SAUCES AND SIDE DISHES

Chicken Stock
Makes 4 litres

2.5 kg raw chicken bones, chopped
3–4 celery sticks
2 leeks
1 onion
1–2 carrots
4 garlic cloves, chopped
5 litres cold water

Put the chicken bones in a large pot with the water and bring to the boil and skim off residue.

Chop the vegetables roughly and add to the pot with garlic. Bring back to the boil and skim. Simmer for 3-4 hours.

Pass through a fine sieve. Chill and store in the fridge until needed. This will keep for up to one week.

Vegetable Stock

Make as Chicken Stock without chicken bones.

Fish Stock
Makes 1 1/3 litres

1 kg fish bones – turbot, monk, lemon sole, brill (not oily fish such as salmon or mackerel)
2 litres water
2-3 sprigs thyme
1 onion, chopped
1 leek, chopped
1 bulb fennel, chopped
1 carrot, chopped
2-3 bay leaves

Place fish bones in cold water. Bring to boil and simmer for 15-20 minutes. Strain into clean pot, add vegetables and herbs and bring back to boil. Simmer for 20-25 minutes. Strain, chill and use as required.

Beef or Veal Stock
Makes 7 litres

2 1/2 kg beef or veal knuckle bones
120ml olive oil
2 onions, peeled and chopped
5 carrots, chopped
3 celery stalks, chopped
Half head garlic, cloves peeled
6 tablespoons tomato purée
Half bottle red wine
10 litres hot water
1 sprig thyme
1 bay leaf

Cook the bones in 4 tablespoons of
oil until golden brown, stirring
occasionally.
In a separate pan, cook the onion,
carrot, celery and garlic in
2 tablespoons oil until golden brown
and add the tomato purée.
When the bones are golden brown, place
in a large stock pot and cover with the
hot water. Bring to the boil and skim.
Add the vegetables and herbs to the
bones and bring back to the boil.
Skim, allow to simmer for 4-5 hours.
Pass through a fine sieve and boil to
reduce by half.
Cool, then store in the fridge.
Will keep for one week.

Lamb Stock
Makes 2 litres

3kg raw lamb bones
2 tablespoons vegetable oil
2 onions
2 celery stalks
2 carrots
1 leek, roughly chopped
4 tablespoons tomato purée
1 full head garlic, cloves peeled
700ml water

Chop the lamb bones, then roast them
in 1 tablespoon oil in a tray on the hob
until golden brown. Drain well.
Sweat the vegetables in the
remaining oil.
Add the tomato purée and the garlic
and cook for 4–5 minutes.
Add the lamb bones to the vegetables.
Cover with water and bring to the boil.
Skim the fat off thoroughly.
Add the herbs and cook the stock at
a fast simmer for 1 hour, skimming
regularly.
Pass through a sieve, chill and keep
in the fridge.
This will last for up to one week.

Tomato Sauce

This can be used for pasta dishes and is also delicious spread on toast for a version of tapas. Good on pizza bases too.

75g carrots, diced
75g onion, diced
2 garlic cloves, peeled and crushed
25ml olive oil
35g plain flour
10g Parma or Serrano dried ham, chopped
400g tomatoes, skinned, de-seeded and chopped
(tinned tomatoes are also suitable)
50g unsalted butter
Salt & freshly ground white pepper

Soften the carrot, onion and garlic in the oil for a few minutes over a medium heat without browning. Stir in the flour and cook gently for 15-20 minutes.
Add the ham and tomatoes to the pan and bring the mixture to the boil.
Add salt and pepper to taste, cover and cook steadily for 30 minutes.
Blend in a liquidiser.

Hollandaise Sauce

Ideal to serve with fish dishes, it is also the classic sauce for Eggs Benedict and with asparagus. Dip bread into leftovers!

100ml white wine vinegar
10 white peppercorns, lightly crushed
A few parsley stalks
1 shallot, peeled and chopped
50ml water
1 tablespoon white wine
2 egg yolks
Juice half lemon
Salt and cayenne pepper
250g butter

Put the vinegar, peppercorns, parsley stalks and shallot into a small pot and boil to reduce by half. Leave for 4 hours to infuse. Add water and wine and strain. Place egg yolks in a bowl with lemon juice, add salt and cayenne to taste. Gradually whisk in strained vinegar reduction for 10 minutes. Place the bowl over warm pot of water. Add butter gradually, whisking until all has been added. Do not allow to boil. If it curdles, start again with a new egg yolk and add the curdled sauce. It will emulsify and smoothen out again. Keep warm in the bowl over simmering water until needed, but not for more than 30 minutes.

Béarnaise Sauce

Add several stalks of tarragon to the Hollandaise vinegar before boiling, reducing and infusing. Make the sauce and add 25 very finely chopped tarragon leaves before serving.

Sauce Paloise

Add several fresh mint stalks to the Hollandaise vinegar before boiling, reducing and infusing. Make the sauce and add 20 very finely chopped mint leaves to the sauce as you serve, not before.

Sauce Mousseline

Into each 600ml of basic sauce Hollandaise, whisk 300ml of semi-whipped double cream.

Mayonnaise

2 medium eggs
3 teaspoons white wine vinegar
Half teaspoon English mustard
Pinch salt
400ml olive oil
Juice half lemon

Place the eggs in a blender and liquidise for 2 minutes.
Add vinegar, mustard and salt.
Blend for 1 minute.
Slowly add the oil while the motor is running or whisking by hand until it forms a thick cream.
Add the lemon juice and mix well.
Place in a cold airtight jar and store in the fridge until required.

Salsa Verde
Serves 8

1 or 2 cloves garlic, peeled & chopped
20 capers
1 small handful sweet pickled gherkins
5 anchovy fillets
3 large handfuls fresh flat-leafed parsley
2 handfuls fresh basil
1 handful fresh mint
2 tablespoons Dijon mustard
45ml/3 tablespoons red wine vinegar
120ml olive oil
Salt and freshly ground black pepper

Finely chop the capers, gherkins, anchovies and herbs.
Place in a bowl and add the mustard and red wine vinegar.
Slowly stir in the olive oil and then balance the flavours with freshly ground black pepper, and if necessary, sea salt and more red wine vinegar.

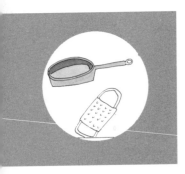

Aïoli
Serves 8

This is a delicious traditional French garlic mayonnaise which makes a tasty accompaniment to fried fish and on bread as a base for toppings. Great with cold rare beef. Extra virgin olive oil is diluted slightly with standard oil to avoid overpowering the final taste, but a mild extra virgin oil can be used instead.

Half small clove garlic, peeled & crushed
Salt and pepper to season
1 large egg yolk
1 teaspoon Dijon mustard
285ml extra virgin olive oil
285ml olive oil
Lemon juice to taste

In a chilled bowl place the egg yolk and mustard and whisk until well blended.
Add the olive oil a little at a time. Once you have blended in half of the olive oil, the rest may be added in greater amounts.
When well blended, add the garlic and lemon.
To finish season to taste with salt, pepper and lemon juice.

Honey dressing

1 dessertspoon honey
1 dessertspoon olive oil
1 dessertspoon vinegar or lemon juice
Salt & freshly ground black pepper
Small teaspoon mustard

Mix all these ingredients to make a
slightly sweet dressing.

Vinaigrette

75ml white wine vinegar
120ml peanut oil
200ml olive oil
Salt & freshly ground white pepper

Put the vinegar in a bowl and add a
pinch salt and pepper.

Add the oils and whisk.

Taste and adjust seasoning if necessary.

Tomato Fondue
Makes about 150ml

This simple mixture is great with fish
dishes, but also with chicken and
turkey leftovers.

6-8 large ripe tomatoes, skinned, de-
seeded and diced (tinned tomatoes are
fine to use off-season)
100ml olive oil
Half shallot, peeled and finely chopped
1 garlic clove, peeled and finely
chopped
1 sprig thyme
Small bay leaf

Heat olive oil in a pan and sweat the
shallot and garlic for 2-3 minutes.
Add the tomato, thyme and bay leaf.
Cook very gently over a low heat until
all the moisture has been removed from
the tomato and what is left is a dry
tomato paste which is full of flavour.
Remove the herbs and buzz the mixture
in a blender until smooth.

Mango, Chilli and Pepper Salsa

This gives a lift to grilled fish, shellfish
or crab cakes and keeps for weeks.

2 whole red peppers
1 mango, peeled and chopped
1 clove garlic, finely chopped
4 red onions, finely chopped
3 chillis, de-seeded and finely chopped
130ml olive oil
1 tablespoon red wine vinegar
3 tablespoons parsley, chopped
6 basil leaves, finely chopped
Salt and black pepper

Grill the peppers, turning at intervals
until the skin has blackened (7–10
minutes).
Skin and de-seed and chop finely.
Mix all the ingredients together.
Season with salt and pepper.
Leave for 2-3 hours to allow flavours
to infuse.

Basil Oil

Basil Pesto

Delicious for simple marinades and as a dressing for salads with a squeeze of lemon juice or a splash of balsamic vinegar. It will keep for 2–3 weeks.

150g basil leaves
2 tablespoons water
220ml olive oil
Salt and black pepper
1 clove garlic, crushed

Purée the basil and water in a blender. Add oil and garlic and seasoning. Chill. Place in an air-tight jar.

This is a versatile sauce and can be used as a base for bruschetta, tapas, pizzas and as a dip. Good with fish and ideal to serve over hot pasta for a simple and quick meal. A few chopped fresh tomatoes make a pasta dish even better. Add a little to mashed potatoes for a change.

4 cloves garlic, crushed
50g pine nuts
130ml olive oil
150g basil leaves
30g Parmesan
Salt and pepper

Put garlic, pine nuts and olive oil into a blender and process until smooth. Add basil leaves, Parmesan, salt and pepper and process until the leaves are completely incorporated. Chill until needed.

Onion Marmalade
Makes approx. 250g

5 medium red onions, finely sliced
Half bottle red wine
1 tablespoon grenadine syrup
25g butter
3 tablespoons red wine vinegar

Soften butter in a deep pan.
Add all other ingredients.
Stir well and cook until all liquid has
evaporated and the onions have a shiny
purple colour.
Allow to cool and place in a sealed jar
and refrigerate.
Lasts for two weeks.

Mrs Coyle's Crabapple Jelly

Gather the apples as soon as they are ripe; don't wait for them all to fall.

Rinse them in a sink of cold water, picking them over for mushy bits, discard these or cut them out.

Empty apples into a large saucepan (no more than half-way up the side) cover with fresh, cold water and bring to the boil, stirring now and again.

When all the apples have burst and are mushy take them off the heat and spoon into a jelly-bag. Suspend this overnight. Do not squeeze as this will make the jelly cloudy.

Next day, measure out the apple liquid and for every litre allow a kilo of white sugar. Pour the apple liquid into a large, clean saucepan, bring to the boil and add the sugar, stirring well to dissolve. Keep boiling and stirring till setting point is reached. Test either by waiting till the last drop on a stirred wooden spoon does not drop but holds on, or until a small spoonful on a saucer left in the fridge till cool forms a skin when pushed with a finger.

Pour into sterilized jars (a jam funnel is a great help and avoids sticky rims) and cover with waxed discs and screw-top lids or cellophane discs as desired. This produces a beautiful jelly of clear rose colour, good with pork, cold meats but especially on hot bread or toast.

Crabapples freeze well, but use only the prettiest, and are a lovely accompaniment to turkey, chicken and pork. Put straight from freezer into roasting pan with a joint of pork, a chicken or turkey for the last 10-15 minutes of cooking.

Remove carefully and place around roast on serving dish.

Herb Crust

80g fresh breadcrumbs
40g Gruyère cheese, grated
25g parsley, chopped
Half teaspoon dill, chopped
60g butter
Salt & freshly ground white pepper

Place all the ingredients into a food
processor and blend until thoroughly
mixed. Use straight away, or freeze.
To freeze, spread out on a lined tray
with greaseproof paper.

Couscous

350g couscous
150ml chicken stock (p.90)
2 red peppers, de-seeded and diced
3 shallots, peeled and diced
100ml olive oil
Juice 2 lemons
1 teaspoon mint, chopped
1 teaspoon coriander, chopped
Salt & freshly ground white pepper

Place the couscous in a bowl and pour
over the boiling chicken stock. Mix so
that the couscous is moistened and
swells.
Mix in the pepper and shallots, olive oil
and lemon juice and season with salt
and pepper. Mix in the herbs.
Serve with salads and chicken dishes.

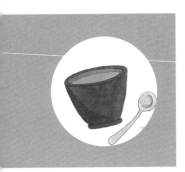

Fresh Pasta
Serves 4-6

600g plain white flour
4 medium eggs
6 egg yolks
1 tablespoon olive oil
Pinch salt

Place the flour in a food processor, and switch the machine on. Slowly add the eggs and egg yolks using the pulse button.
Add the olive oil and salt and mix briefly.
Remove from the machine and knead for a few minutes on a lightly floured surface until even and smooth.
Divide into 8 equal pieces, cover with cling film, and allow to rest for at least an hour before rolling and cutting as appropriate.
Any pasta not to be used straightaway can be frozen.
If using a pasta machine, it is easy to roll out thinly and cut into strips. Otherwise, work by hand and use a rolling pin to roll the dough paper thin. Cut into strips, or rectangles for lasagne, circles for ravioli.
To cook, drop into boiling salted water for 30 seconds, refresh in cold water and drain.

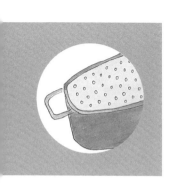

Puy Lentils

Suitable for Guinea fowl, chicken dishes and plain fried fish. Also good with cold roasted lamb.

225g Puy lentils
1 sprig thyme
Small bay leaf
1 garlic clove, peeled
1 litre chicken stock
15g unsalted butter
25g smoked bacon, diced
25g carrot, diced
25g celery, diced
25g shallot, diced
Salt & freshly ground white pepper

Soak the lentils in water for 8 hours.
Drain and place in a pan with the thyme, bay, garlic and enough stock to cover.
Bring to the boil and simmer for 10 minutes.
Drain the lentils, remove herbs and garlic and leave to cool.
Heat the butter in a large frying pan over a moderate heat and add the bacon and diced vegetables. Sweat gently until soft. Add the lentils and cook gently to warm them through. Season to taste.

Polenta Cake with Herbs

Polenta requires quite a lot of elbow grease to beat, so make it on an energetic day. Tim's recipes ensures that the effort is worthwhile.

500g polenta
180ml cream
500ml milk
20g butter
2 shallots, finely chopped
1 clove garlic, crushed
1 cup chopped chives, basil, coriander and chervil

Heat the milk, butter, shallots and garlic in a heavy-based pan. Bring to the boil, then reduce the heat to a simmer. Slowly add the polenta in a thin stream, stirring constantly.
Continue to simmer on a low heat, stirring until the mixture is thick and comes away from the sides of the pan. This will take 35-40 minutes.
Stir in the herbs.
Allow to cool. Spread out into a 3cm deep tray and leave to set. Cut out rounds or square using a 5cm cutter.
To serve, reheat in oven, shallow fry in olive oil or grill both sides until golden.

Confit of Garlic

Garlic Mash
Serves 4-6

Confit means preserve and often refers to duck which is cooked in its own fat, cooled and stored, covered in fat. Here, Tim cooks garlic in duck fat which seals it to keep air out. It livens up any roast meat and is good with grilled tomatoes and simply on toast.

12-16 large cloves garlic, unpeeled
100g goose fat
2 bay leaves
2 small sprigs thyme

Half fill a small saucepan with the goose fat and place on the stove to heat until warm. Add the bay leaves, thyme and garlic. Cook for 20–30 minutes, remove from heat and allow to cool. Keep the garlic and goose fat in the fridge. To serve: Remove from the fat, peel and fry in a dry pan to crisp up. Use as a garnish for meat or fish.

10 large potatoes, peeled and cubed
Pinch salt
3 cloves garlic, crushed
80g butter
220ml cream

Put the potatoes in a pot of salted water. Bring to the boil and cook for 25 minutes.
Drain, mash and transfer to a bowl. Rinse out pot, add cream and garlic and cook until it has reduced by one-third. Add butter and allow to melt. Add the cream mixture to the potatoes and mix. Reheat and season if necessary.

Courgettes with Almonds

This is a good way to make the best
of courgettes when in season. The fried
courgettes make a good contrast in
texture and taste to the cream and
browned almonds.

500g courgettes
40g plain flour
4 dessertspoons olive oil
20g butter
120ml cream
40g sliced almonds
2 tablespoons chopped chives
Salt and pepper
10ml lemon juice

Trim the ends of the courgettes and cut
into 2cm strips. Dip in flour.
Heat the oil and butter in a pan and
add the courgettes in small amounts at
a time. Cook until golden brown. Drain
on kitchen paper. Keep warm.
Add the almonds to the pan, cook until
brown, stir in the cream and lemon
juice. Season to taste and heat gently.
Place the courgettes in a serving dish.
Garnish with cream, almonds and
chopped chives on top.

Parsnip and Honey Bake

This is a perfect accompaniment to
roast lamb or duck and makes an interesting change with turkey. Vegetarians
will enjoy this as a substantial main
course, served with salad

600g parsnips
70g butter
2 large onions, sliced
2 medium eggs
100ml cream
5 slices brown bread
2 tablespoons honey
50g sesame seeds
Salt and pepper

Preheat oven to 200°c/400f/Gas 6.

Wash and peel the parsnips, cut into
thin slices. Boil in salted water for
15 minutes and drain.
Melt butter in a pot, add onion and fry
until lightly browned.
Blend the onions, parsnips, eggs,
cream and honey in a food processor
and season.
Butter an ovenproof dish, cover the
base with the sliced bread and spoon in
the parsnip mix. Sprinkle with sesame
seeds. Bake in oven for 25-30 minutes
until golden brown.

Carrots with Mint, Lemon and Garlic

Lemon and garlic make a perfect match with lamb, and carrots are in season at just the right time. Serve with roast leg or shank of lamb, crisply roasted chicken, cold turkey, beef kebabs and fish dishes.

Serves 4-6

600g carrots, peeled
1 lemon, juice and rind
1 teaspoon brown sugar
1 tablespoon olive oil
15-20 leaves mint, finely chopped
1 clove garlic, crushed
Salt and black pepper
2 tablespoons fresh parsley, chopped

Cut carrots into 5cm chunks. Cook in boiling, salted water for 15-20 minutes and drain.
Heat oil in a large pan, add garlic and cook for 1 minute on a medium heat.
Add carrots, lemon, sugar and mint.
Cook for 4-5 minutes. Season.
Transfer to a serving dish and sprinkle with chopped parsley.

Basil Mash

10-12 large potatoes, peeled and cubed
8-10 basil leaves, shredded
Salt & pepper
80g butter
200ml cream

Put the potatoes in a pot of salted water. Bring to the boil and cook for 25 minutes.
Drain, mash and transfer to a bowl.
Rinse out pot and add cream and basil and cook until it has reduced by one-third.
Add butter and allow to melt. Add this to the potatoes and mix.
Reheat and season if necessary.

Puréed Potatoes

This simple and delicious creamed potato can also be used for scallion mash by
adding 4 chopped scallions to the cream
before heating. Tim favours Roosters for
mashing and roasting, with Golden
Wonders as second choice for flavour
and texture.

10-12 medium potatoes, washed, peeled
and cubed
Salt & pepper
80g butter
200ml cream

Put the potatoes in a pot with salted
water. Bring to the boil and cook for 25
minutes.

Drain, mash and transfer to a bowl.
Heat cream, reduce by one-third, add
butter and allow to melt.

Add the cream mixture to the potatoes
and mix. Reheat and season to taste.

Crème Patissière

6 medium egg yolks
75g caster sugar
50g plain flour
400ml milk

In a pan, cream the egg yolks and sugar
together well, then mix in the flour.

Bring the milk to the boil in another
pan then whisk a little into the egg
yolks.

Add the remainder of the liquid and
cook over a gentle heat, stirring to a
smooth cream for no longer than
5 minutes.

Use as a base in fruit tartlets.

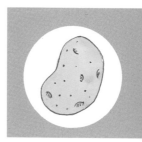

Crème Anglaise

This classic sauce for puddings
and tartlets is a light vanilla custard.

6 medium egg yolks
120g caster sugar
500ml milk
1 vanilla pod (optional)

Mix the egg yolks and sugar together
in a bowl.

Bring the milk and the vanilla to the
boil in a pan. Pour the hot milk into
the egg yolks in the bowl and mix well.
Then return the milk to the pan.
Cook very slowly over a gentle heat,
stirring constantly, until the mixture
thickens. Remove from the heat and
pass through a fine sieve into a bowl.
Leave to chill.

Coffee Crème Anglaise
Add 20g instant coffee powder, diluted
in a little water, to the basic crème
anglaise

Liqueur Crème Anglaise
Add a liqueur - Grand Marnier is a
favourite - to the basic crème anglaise.

Passion-Fruit Sauce

250g passion-fruit pulp (about
12 fruits)
30g caster sugar
1 tablespoon water
3 tablespoons fresh orange juice
85ml stock syrup *see right*

Put the passion-fruit pulp and seeds in
a saucepan with the caster sugar and
water. Bring the mixture to the boil and
simmer for 2-3 minutes.
Liquidise the mixture briefly and pass
it through a fine sieve, leaving the
seeds behind.
Add the juice and syrup to the sieved
pulp and bring to the boil. Sieve and
chill.

Stock Syrup

450g caster sugar
600ml water
3 cinnamon sticks

Put the sugar, water and cinnamon
sticks in a pot and bring to the boil
slowly. Cook over a low heat for
5 minutes.

Christmas at Renvyle

Christmas is special at Renvyle with a most warming ambience

and hospitality. Tim's food is traditional, but always has its surprises, with

a flourish and unique quality that is difficult to describe. Perhaps it is all

about good taste from top quality ingredients, enjoyed by those who would

not miss a Renvyle Christmas and return every year for more of the same.

He says these recipes are simple, which is true, but it is wise to stay close

to proportions as balance is the key.

Traditional Roast Turkey   Serves 6

6kg oven-ready turkey
1kg apricot, thyme and parsley stuffing
(see p.115)
50g butter
Salt and black pepper.

Preheat the oven to 200°c/400°f/
Gas 6.

Rub the skin of the turkey with the
butter and season with salt and pepper.

Place the stuffing into the body cavity
of the turkey and secure with skewers.
Place the turkey on a roasting tray and
cover lightly with foil.

Place in the oven and baste every hour.
Cook for 3-4 hours. For the last 30 minutes, remove the foil so the skin
becomes crisp.

Remove from the oven and leave to rest
for 10 minutes before carving.

Roast Goose

Serves 6

4-5kg oven-ready goose
500g boiled potatoes
1 onion
85g butter
2 tablespoons chopped fresh sage
1 tablespoon chopped fresh thyme
2 tablespoons chopped fresh parsley
300g black pudding, minced
Half lemon
Salt and black pepper

Preheat the oven to 200°c/400°f/
Gas 6.

Prick the goose all over.

Squeeze the juice of the half lemon into
the cavity and sprinkle with salt.

Mash the potatoes.

Melt the butter in a saucepan and fry
the onion until soft, add the black pudding, thyme, parsley, sage and potatoes.
Cook for 2-3 minutes.

Stuff the goose with the mixture and
secure with skewers. Place the goose on
a rack in a large roasting tin and cook
for 40 minutes. Reduce the temperature
to 180°c/350°f/Gas 4 and continue
cooking for 2-3 hours.

Remove from oven and leave to rest for
10 minutes before carving.
Serve with roasted vegetables.

Apricot, Thyme and Parsley Stuffing

1 clove garlic, crushed
180g butter
2 shallots, diced
550g white breadcrumbs
Juice and zest of half lemon
3 tablespoons chopped thyme
3 tablespoons chopped parsley
150g dried apricots, diced
Salt and pepper

Melt butter in a saucepan over a medium heat and cook garlic and shallots until soft.
Add all the other ingredients and cook for a further 2-3 minutes.
Season with salt and pepper

Port and Cranberry Sauce

1 shallot, finely diced
1 clove garlic, crushed
165ml chicken stock
Juice and zest of 1 orange
3 tablespoons redcurrant jelly
100g fresh cranberries
Half glass port
80g butter

Melt 40g butter in a saucepan over a medium heat, add shallots and garlic and cook until soft.
Add port and reduce for 1-2 minutes.
Add chicken stock, zest and juice of the orange and cook for 12–15 minutes
Add the cranberries and redcurrant jelly. Simmer for 5–8 minutes.
Whisk in the remaining butter and season to taste.
Serve with Roast Turkey or Roast Goose.

Baked Ham with Cider and Cloves

2kg smoked ham
50g brown sugar
15-20 cloves
320ml cider

Preheat the oven to 200°c/
400°f/Gas 6.

Place the ham in a pot of water
and simmer, covered, for 2 to 3
hours. Remove from the pot and
allow to cool.

Reduce cider in a pot and add
sugar to make a syrup.

Remove fat from ham and stud
with cloves.

Place ham in a roasting tray and
coat with syrup. Bake in the oven
for 25 minutes.Remove and keep
warm until serving.

Brussels Sprouts with Smoked Bacon

600g Brussels sprouts, trimmed
6 slices of smoked bacon, cut
into strips
1 medium onion, diced
50g butter
1 clove garlic, crushed
Salt & pepper
Olive oil

Cook sprouts in boiling salted
water for 4 to 6 minutes. Drain.
Heat oil in a pan and fry bacon,
garlic and onion for 2 to 3
minutes.
Add sprouts and butter and cook
for 1 to 2 minutes.
Season with salt and pepper.

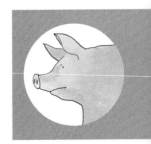

Roast Vegetables in a Parcel

Ideally choose Rooster potatoes
for this dish as they will not fall
apart during baking and have a
good flavour.

1 turnip
3 carrots
2 parsnips
1 onion, sliced
5 potatoes
4 cloves garlic
10 sprigs thyme
Olive oil
Sea salt
Black pepper

Preheat the oven to 220°f/425°f
/Gas 7.

Line a roasting tray with tin foil.

Wash and peel the vegetables and
potatoes. Cut into large wedges.
Peel and slice the garlic.

Sprinkle some olive oil on the
base of the tray. Place the carrots
on the bottom, sprinkle with sea
salt and pepper, some garlic
and thyme.

Layer with parsnips, garlic and
thyme. Add the potatoes, turnips
and onion with the remaining
garlic and thyme. Add some sea
salt and pepper and a good coating of olive oil.

Fold the tin foil over to make a
parcel, place in the oven and bake
for 1 hour and 10 minutes. They
will keep hot for 20 minutes, if
necessary.

Mince Pies

450g mincemeat
1 egg white
Caster sugar
Shortcrust pastry

Shortcrust Pastry:
200g plain flour
Half teaspoon salt
50g lard
50g margarine
2 tablespoons water

Preheat oven to 220°c/425°f
/Gas 7.

Sieve the flour and salt into
a bowl.

Cut the lard and margarine into
small cubes (1.5cm) and rub into
the flour.

Make a well in the centre and add
the water, mixing to produce a
soft dough. Wrap in clingfilm or
foil and chill until required.

Mincemeat

100g cooking apples, peeled
and chopped
70g raisins
70g sultanas
50g currants
35g mixed peel
70g brown sugar
70g suet, finely chopped
10g chopped almonds
Juice and rind of half lemon
Half teaspoon mixed spice
1 tablespoon brandy

Mince coarsely the apples, raisins,
currants, sultanas and mixed peel.
Place in a bowl and add the sugar,
suet, almonds, lemon juice and
rind, mixed spice and brandy. Mix
all together.

This can be made one week in
advance. Store in tightly sealed
jars.

To finish the pies:
Roll the pastry thinly and cut into
rounds about 8cm for the pie
bases.

Line patty tins with these and fill
about half their depth with mincemeat.
Cut out slightly smaller rounds
for the covers. Dampen the rims
of the pie bases with cold water
and place the cover on top, press-
ing the edges together lightly to
seal them.

Make a small slit in the top of
each pie, brush with egg white
and sprinkle with caster sugar.
Place in the oven and bake for
20 minutes.

Remove and allow to stand for
2 to 3 minutes before removing
from the tins.

Serve with whipped cream
flavoured with vanilla.

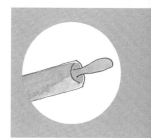

Christmas Pudding

225g white breadcrumbs
225g shredded suet
225g self-raising flour
350g sultanas
225g currants
350g raisins
225g brown sugar
1 teaspoon salt
2 teaspoons mixed spice
125g mixed peel
150g glacé cherries
1 red apple, peeled and grated
6 eggs, beaten
Grated rind and juice of 1 orange
Grated rind and juice of 1 lemon
300ml stout

Grease three 1 litre pudding basins.

Mix flour, suet, breadcrumbs, dried fruit and sugar together in a bowl.

Add the salt, mixed spice, mixed peel, cherries and the grated apple. Mix together.

In a separate bowl mix the eggs, orange and lemon juice, the rind and the stout. Add to the dry ingredients and mix.

Divide the mixture between the three basins.

Cover each basin with greaseproof paper and tie with string and place each in a pot of boiling water. The water level should be halfway up the pudding basin.

Cover the pots with lids and steam for at least 6 hours. Top up with boiling water to maintain the water level.

When cooked remove the basins and leave to cool. Pour some brandy over each pudding, re-cover with fresh greaseproof paper and store in a cool, dry place.

Before serving, cover with fresh greaseproof paper and steam again for 3 hours. Serve with brandy sauce.

Brandy Sauce

75g butter
75g caster sugar
300ml cream
4 tablespoons brandy

Combine all the ingredients in a saucepan
over a low heat for 2 to 3 minutes, then
bring to the boil for 3 to 4 minutes. Remove
from heat and keep warm.

Broad beans

french bea

nner beans

Angela
Kane

Susie-May
Walsh

Zoë
Fitzgerald

Aoife
Halde

Laura
Verdilton

Alex
Kane

Thibauld
Mialet

Emilee
Pelloquin

Michael
Cannina

Tim
O'Sulliva

All at Renvyle, photographed noon friday 15 july 2005

Niall viney   Mathew Adam   Samuel le Cam   Bastien Sawatzki   Ronnie Counihan   Katarzyna Trubilowicz   Emma O'Sullivan   Peter Malaski

Off-duty on the day: John D Coyle (Chairman & Owner), Sabina Flaherty, Marty Hilsden, Thomas Coyne, Daniel Flaherty, Mary Horkan, Fiona Joyce, Catherine Mulholland, Aingeal Mylotte, Carmel O' Sullivan, Tracy Folan, Helena Coyne, Sadie Coyne, Celia Flaherty, Kathleen Kane, Sorcha Geary, Geraldine Hannon, Annabel Kane, John Francis Hannon

126   Index

aïoli 94
almond, and cauliflower soup 35
almonds with courgettes 105
angel hair pasta with killary bay prawns 15
anglaise, crème 108
apple and onion soup 37
apricot and herb stuffing 54
apricot and pear filo roulade 71
apricot, thyme and parsley stuffing 115
asparagus 49
asparagus soup 42
aubergine and tomato lasagne 67
aubergine, toasted 62
bacon, smoked and cabbage 61
baguette, garlic 18
baked beetroot 46
baked ham 116
basil and vegetable provencale 48
basil mash 106
basil oil 97
basil pesto 97
bass, pan-seared 45
beans, green 49
béarnaise sauce 93
beef stock 91
beetroot, baked 46
beetroot and chive dressing 51
beetroot and walnut dressing 60
beurre blanc, chive 52
black sole fillets 50
blue cheese and broccoli soup 39
brandy sauce 121
bread and butter pudding 81
bread, brown soda 85
bread, oatmeal and buttermilk 85
bread, yeast 84
breast of duckling 62
brill, steamed in red pepper sauce 48
broccoli and blue cheese soup 39
brown soda bread 85
brulée, crème 74
brussels sprouts 116
butter and bread pudding 81
butter, garlic and tomato 49
butter, lemon and tomato sauce 47
buttermilk and oatmeal bread 85
butternut squash risotto 52
cabbage and smoked bacon 61

cabbage, crispy green 62
cake, ginger 87
cake, polenta with herbs 102
cakes, west coast crab 27
carrot and orange soup 38
carrots with mint, lemon and garlic 106
cauliflower and almond soup 35
cauliflower and spinach, creamed 50
cauliflower purée 50
cheese, goat's salad 24
chicken breast, corn-fed 58
chicken liver paté 20
chicken mousse with tarragon 19
chicken stock 90
chicken vegetable terrine 16
chilli mango and pepper salsa 96
chilli sauce 62
chive and beetroot dressing 51
chive beurre blanc sauce 52
chocolate, dark mousse 80
chocolate steamed puddings 76
chowder, seafood 40
christmas pudding 120
coconut and curry cream 27
cod, fillet 47
coffee crème anglaise 108
confit of garlic 103
connemara lamb 54
connemara lobster 49
connemara scallops 52
connemara smoked fish platter 26
courgettes with almonds 105
couscous 100
couscous, savoury 22
crab cakes, west coast 27
crabapple jelly, mrs coyle's 99
crabmeat, tower of 16
cranberry and port sauce 115
creamed spinach and cauliflower 50
crème anglaise 108
crème brulée 74
crème fraiche, curried 28
crème patissière 107
crisps, parsnip 46
crispy breast of duckling 62
crispy green cabbage 62
crumble, rhubarb and ginger 72
crust, herb 100
curried crème fraiche 28
curry and coconut cream 27
dark and white chocolate mousse 79
dark chocolate mousse 80
dressing, chive and beetroot 51
dressing, honey 95
duck spring roll 22

duckling breast 62
fillet steaks 59
filo, pear and apricot roulade 71
fish stock 90
fish, bass 45
fish, connemara smoked platter 26
fondue, tomato 96
fresh pasta 101
fruit scones 87
garlic and spinach timbale 53
garlic and tomato butter 49
garlic baguette 18
garlic confit 103
garlic mash 103
garlic, with carrots and lemon 106
ginger and rhubarb crumble 72
ginger cake 87
ginger, with lemongrass and mussels 14
goat's cheese, rocket, red pepper salsa 214
goose, roast 114
gravy, rosemary 55
green beans 49
ham, baked 116
herb and apricot stuffing 54
herb crust 100
hollandaise sauce 92
honey and parsnip bake 105
honey dressing 95
ice-cream, pistachio 72
irish stew 57
jelly, mrs coyle's crabapple 99
lamb connemara 54
lamb shanks 56
lamb stock 91
lasagne, aubergine and tomato 67
leek and shallot tart 66
leeks, creamed 47
lemon butter and tomato sauce 47
lemon, with carrots and garlic 106
lemongrass, with ginger and mussels 14
lentils, puy 101
lentils, with chicken 58
liqueur crème anglaise 108
liver, chicken paté 20
lobster, connemara 49
mango, chill and pepper salsa 96
marmalade, onion 98
mash, basil 106
mash, garlic 103
mayonnaise 93
mince pies 19
mincemeat 119
mint, in carrots with lemon and garlic 106
mixed salad leaves 28,16
mousse, chicken with tarragon 19

mousse, dark and white chocolate 79
mousse, dark chocolate 80
mousseline sauce 93
mozzarella and grilled tomato salad 21
mrs coyle's crabapple jelly 99
mushroom and red wine sauce 59
mushroom soup 34
mushroom, wild cream 59
mussels, saffron 46
mussels, with lemongrass and ginger 14
oatmeal and buttermilk bead 85
oil, basil 97
onion and apple soup 37
onion marmalade 98
onion, spring salsa 16
orange and carrot soup 38
oyster soup 33
paloise sauce 93
pan-roasted quail 60
pan-seared bass 45
parsley, apricot and thyme stuffing 115
parsnip and honey bake 105
parsnip crisps 46
passion-fruit and vanilla crème brulée 74
passion-fruit sauce 109
pasta, angel hair with killary bay
prawns 15
pasta, fresh 101
paté, chicken liver 20
pear and apricot filo roulade 71
pepper and rocket salsa 24
pepper mango and chilli salsa 96
pepper, yellow cream 46
pesto, basil 97
pheasant with smoked bacon 64
pies, mince 119
pineapple and spring onion salsa 22
pistachio ice-cream 72
polenta cake with herbs 102
port and cranberry sauce 115
port and redcurrant sauce 61
potatoes, puréed 107
prawns, with angel hair pasta 15
pudding, bread and butter 81
pudding, christmas 120
puddings, steamed chocolate 76
purée, cauliflower 50
puréed potatoes 107
puy lentils 101
quail, pan-roasted 60
ratatouille 54
red pepper sauce 48
red peppers, in garlic baguette 18
red wine and mushroom sauce 59
renvyle salad with smoked tuna 25

renvyle seafood chowder 40
rhubarb and ginger crumble 72
roast goose 114
roast vegetables in a parcel 117
roasted tomato and mozzarella salad 21
roasted tomatoes 50
rocket and pepper salsa 24
rosemary gravy 55
roulade of the sea 28
roulade, pear and apricot filo 71
saffron mussels 46
salad leaves, mixed 16, 28
salad, goat's cheese 24
salad, renvyle with smoked tuna 25
salmon, smoked with cod 47
salsa verde 94
salsa, mango, chill and pepper 96
salsa, rocket and pepper 24
salsa, spring onion 16
salsa, spring onion and pineapple 22
sauce béarnaise 93
sauce, brandy 121
sauce hollandaise 92
sauce mousseline 93
sauce paloise 93
sauce, passion-fruit 109
sauce, port and cranberry 115
sauce, port and redcurrant 61
sauce, red pepper 48
sauce, red wine and mushroom 59
sauce, sweet chilli 62
sauce, tomato 92
savoury couscous 22
scallops, connemara 52
scones, fruit 87
seafood chowder 40
seafood roulade 28
serrano ham in garlic baguette 18
shallot and leek tart 66
shanks of lamb 56
smoked bacon and cabbage 60
smoked fish platter 26
smoked salmon with fillet of cod 47
smoked tuna with renvyle salad 25
soda, brown bread 85
sole, back fillets 50
soup, apple and onion 37
soup, asparagus 42
soup, broccoli and blue cheese 39
soup, carrot and orange 38
soup, cauliflower and almond 35
soup, mushroom 34
soup, oyster 33
soup, renvyle seafood chowder 40
spicy stir-fried vegetables 22

spinach and garlic timbale 53
spinach, creamed with cauliflower 50
spring onion and pineapple salsa 22
spring onion salsa 15
springroll of duck 22
sprouts, brussels with smoked bacon 116
squash, butternut risotto 52
steamed brill in red pepper sauce 48
steamed chocolate pudding 76
stew, irish 58
stir-fried vegetables 22
stock syrup 109
stock, beef 91
stock, chicken 90
stock, fish 90
stock, lamb 91
stock, veal 91
stock, vegetable 90
stuffing for goose 115
stuffing, herb and apricot 54
sweet chilli sauce 62
syrup stock 109
tarragon, chicken mousse with 19
tart, shallot and leek 66
terrine, chicken and vegetable 16
thyme, apricot and parsley stuffing 115
toasted aubergine 62
tomato and aubergine lasagne 67
tomato and garlic butter 49
tomato and lemon butter sauce 47
tomato fondue 96
tomato sauce 92
tomato, grilled salad with mozzarella 21
tomatoes, roasted 50
tower of crabmeat, 16
traditional toast turkey 113
tuna, smoked with renvyle salad 25
turkey, roast 113
vanilla and passion-fruit crème brulée 74
veal stock 91
vegetable and basil provencale 48
vegetable chicken terrine 16
vegetable stock 90
vegetables, roast in a parcel 117
vegetables, spicy stir-fried 22
venison 61
verde salsa 94
vinaigrette 95
walnut and beetroot dressing 60
west coast crab cakes 27
white and dark chocolate mousse 79
wild mushroom cream 58
wine, red and mushroom sauce 59
yeast bread 84
yellow pepper cream 46